<u>1000</u>

I speak in 1000 rhymes.
I've lived over 1000 times.
So, I feel like I've written 1000 lines from 1000 minds.
Rise and shine with clear mind...
Rebirthed on planet Earth.
As 1000 pages unfold from 1000 stories never told.

"They should've sent a poet." – Jodi Foster, *Contact*

Continuum:

A collection of poetry
by Joann C. Roberts

In Gratitude

A continuum is defined as something that keeps going and changing over time, a coherent whole made up of many parts that is always present. The Universe, the cosmos is a continuum and so are we. Given this timelessness I decided to gather all poems from previously published books as well as my latest writings to create an anthology. This book contains over 300 poems spanning nearly twenty years -- dating back to my earliest writings at the age of 13, to today -- the post-Saturn Return of my early thirties.

I write through captivity and freedom, darkness and light, confusion and clarity, my feminine and masculine, love and pain. There are poems in this book I never thought could be written, yet alone performed or published. Yet, here we are. My pen demands space wherever I am unwelcome, writing outside the lines of time and reason. My pen is self-critical and honest. It is my healing and my claim to liberation. Just like you and I, my pen is earthly flawed and cosmically flawless.

Saturn Returns are all about letting go, learning important lessons, and allowing aspects of Self to be destroyed for the purposes of rebuilding someone better, stronger. I am closing chapters and making way for anew, as both my art and I continue on beyond this book. With that said, welcome to the first part of the continuum. Throughout our shared experience of space and time, I know there is a poem somewhere in these pages for you. Thank you for turning them.

Table of Contents

Quantum
(Love Mechanics)

The Desire Continuum

She has the smoothest skin I've never touched.

<u>Goddess</u>

She has the smoothest skin I've never touched.
The softest hands I've never clutched.
A body I've never held,
Yet I feel well versed in such.
When it comes to matters of the heart
This woman is a gentle soul.
Leaving me speechless as a weakness
Despite every mental note.
She has silky hair I've never brushed.
Her brown eyes can be too much.
Enough
To make you question Life...
The Who's, Ands, Ifs, and What's.
Something about her feels so warm
Like clouds breaking after a storm.
Where rose petals begin to form
And, the soil beneath us is reborn.
These are things that can't be explained
Only flowed with as they happen.
For this is Love in the times of science
Wrapped in the scent of a woman's satin.
Eye have only seen her once
But feel I've known her before.
Like gravity of the Moon within
Or the depths of ocean floors.
She has a voice I've never heard.
Speaks a language I've never learned.
Yet energy is universal
And when eye saw her eye discerned...
That she's the smoothest skin I've never touched.
The softest hands I've never clutched.
She loves in a way I've never known
And yet I feel well versed in such.

The Way It Should Be

There's no explanation for this situation
I hold within my hands.
This complication of communication...
not even Love itself can understand.
And given the circumstances
I know I have only slimed my chances.
For not even the best of novels and movies
can make sense of these romances.
I simply crave your enchantment.
Such an enhancement only left me to think.
Frozen in time, you engulf my mind...
Now, no water flows smoothly through this sink.
Yet, still, as a waterfall you remain the freshest,
most purified drink.
I am left with sensations of precipitation from my eyes
with each blink.

You told me I cross your mind sometimes,
Though, we lost our minds sometimes.
Now it's hard to believe or perceive that we were
divine at one time.
And I don't remember lying one time,
Yet, it's the honesty that killed me.
It was by way of truth that you made me feel guilty.
And I used excuses to shield me,
But they only blocked me from you.
The reflection of our direction was simply taken
from your view.
Mirrors see clearer.
These objects are further away than they seem.
Now completely out of reach,
and still you remain my Dream.
We both know Love and time do not belong in the

same sentence.
How I feel for you is endless and no clock exists
for repentance.
Hurt myself over and over for you...
Things got older and older to you...
How naive of me to think my mistakes would bring me
closer and closer to you.

All we have is that moment.
The night you laid in my lap.
I caressed every strand of your hair and ran my hands
across your back.
You made me dinner...Conversed with me...
Rubbed my head while I took a nap.
Such moments last forever,
and time could never end that.
Out of mind when out of sight...Only somewhat true.
Though I am here and you are there,
you know I can still feel you.

And I never got the chance to tell you that I love you.
I don't know what I was afraid of...
For you saw and believed what I was made of.
I apologize for making you wait up...
On those lonely nights for my call.
I had no idea...though, you made it clear...
for me you were prepared to fall.
I had no clue at all, that I was the one building a wall.
You helped me find my voice,
and now we don't even talk.
There is really no need to explain how much
I've grown to miss you.
I am sure sunlight still reflects off of you
as it does crystals.

I don't want any past issues to pick at the wound
of a healing scar.
By far...I must take this chance to honor
the woman you are.

I still want to explore every single inch
of your amazing body.
Probably...Take you to the beach, lay you out,
and caress your feet.
I still want to f--k you...
then make the sweetest love to you.
Promise to never corrupt you,
for, now I know what it does to you.
No need to aim the finger and blame,
for we were both in the wrong.
Can't help but wonder if you think with her
is where you truly belong.
You may wonder what could have been
but I wonder what could be.
Cause no matter how happy you are,
deep down you know where you should be.

Right here with me.

Stone

I know that I am wrong for you, yet I long for you.
In weakest times it repeats in mind...
That I must remain strong for you.
Being drawn to you...
Is what I am inevitably prone to do.
There is nothing greater than my love...
Written in stone for you.

Ghost

She has disappeared from my arms...

Indefinitely.
But I have not let go.
My sensations of her
Keep her in my presence at all times.
I still touch her
Still kiss her
Still taste her...
So vividly.

I still put her face to every queen I see.

I still know her
Still write her
Still crave her...
In fantasy.
I still love her based solely
On memory.
I just want her
Don't need her...
In reality.

Yet every night she still lies next to me...

Invisibly.

Dancefloor (A Story)

She was an amazing woman.
I knew the moment I laid eyes on her.
With eagle eyes, she became my prize
as I entered the room.
Overwhelmed with intimidation.
Thinking of ways I could approach her.
Beauty that made me feel inept.
So, I took slow steps of caution toward her space.
Welcomed with glowing brown eyes
and a smile that melts ice.
I think twice but gain the courage.
She grabs my hand and time slows.
Her energy begins to flow throughout me.
Her aura warmed my heart.
I was far from shy. She made me shy.
I never stutter. She made me stutter.
And from there nothing but substance,
as I tried to hold back with sustenance.
But her words drew me in like dots connecting
in coloring books.
Quid pro quo, as she takes me out onto the floor.
Cultivating a connection.
In coherence, the music serves as our protection.
Suddenly, in a different section, as if we were all alone
in the dark room.
She pirouettes her feet to the bass, guides my hands
among her figure.
She defines class. Exchange laughs.
I rest my chin on her shoulder. Comfort.
Within my arms she is secure. She smelled like heaven.
A natural high. Now I live each day in that moment.
The moment I fell in Love with a complete
stranger. She called me there that night though we
had never met before...
...And I never saw her again.

Do You Believe?

Memories of you still echo
as if they were sent here from yesterday.
And, today I move backwards in time
just to feel you again. You'd have to look through a
telescope to find us. We are lost in shadows of dark
matter that must make way for the Sun.
I've listened to unspoken words and heard only what
you never say. You choose your words carefully but
your hips are lips when they sway.
I write scripts in this mind from stories that have never
been told. Stories we mold into gold...We are much too
young to be this old.
And these scripts replay in slow motion on my many
mental screens...Somewhere in between my dreams
and the last time you were seen.
I forget to remember I love you then I remember to
forget. Storing memories and imaginations of
experiences I've never had yet.
You have beautiful hands. The kind it is impossible to
forget. I am convinced you only touched me to remind
me of the night sky's allure.
We've never been together, but I always felt as though
you were there. You reflected upon my heart like solar
flares in northern air.
So, let us come pass this magnetic force and walk
toward magnetic north. I would follow your compass
anywhere as you encompass my every thought.
Like mind's eye philosophy... you brought out
the God in me. You dominated and submitted to me
in ways that complimented my androgyny.
And, when I can feel you is the only time this confusion
makes sense. So, I lie to myself to find truth in all of this.
A battle of Love and hate...we ended the way we should
have begun. Battle of heart and mind...

End forward...Start behind.
So, can you justify your knowledge
without knowing you know?
Should I really believe you love me
minus the actions to show?
Am I "delusionally" justified in being unjustifiably
infatuated?
Seeking justice in an "unjusticed" system you've only
designed to hold me captive.
Do you believe in Love?
Do you really believe in Love?
That spoken words can be unspoken
only in terms of what has never been said?
Do you believe that if I touched you
it was timelessly for tomorrow?
To remind you of all we did...
scattered among our cosmic grid.
Do you believe in time travel?
That I would risk everything I have
to feel your touches of yesterday
in the many moments of now?
Do you believe that I was willing
to love you one million times over?
To be your rock? Your spine?
Your steel engineered shoulder?
Do you believe that I would please you?
Invade your heart then deceive you?
Kiss you as though to free you...
then I'd make love to you like I need you?
Do you believe you could just surrender...
then remember...to forget?
That I just may love you more than you were
ever willing to accept?
Do you believe in Love?
Do you really believe in Love?

We value yesterdays like gold but we are
much too young to be this old.
And these scripts replay in slow motion
on mental screens...
Somewhere in between my dreams
And, those thighs I'd lie between.
Like beams of light from setting Suns...
You were none other than my reflection.
You wouldn't believe how much it hurts.
You wouldn't believe how much I've questioned.
So, I... strum these chords as a looking backward to
move forward.
For, you are much too self-absorbed to bleed from
these mental swords.
Sometimes, I want to speak on those unspoken words
that were never heard.
But...letters only dissipate in the space between my lips
and a word.
You have beautiful hands.
My locs once flowed through them like grains of sand.
But...you'd have to believe in US to even
begin to understand.

You make me weak.

Space-time

You say anything is possible…

But you need space and time.

Given the space and time…

We will transcend space and time.

Traveling at speeds faster than light.

Immeasurable to man and his physics.

For you and I have no space or time…

For impossibilities.

The Chances

If it were up to you, I'd never see you again.
If it were up to me, I'd see you 1000 x through
magnified optical glass.
But it is not up to us. It is up to "God".

The Wall

Separated we are
By the wall.
Through all the feelings
We still cannot touch each other...
See each other.
Who built this wall?
Why is it keeping us from forever?
We try to break this wall.
We try to climb over this wall.
But this wall is so strong.
This same old wall
Haunts us every time.
I just wish I'd known you
Before we built it.

Eternal

I will light 1000 candles in your heart...
Then walk this Love through the fire of
immortality.
Just give me your hand...
And meet me on the other side.

Stare

I need you to reject me.
These moving pictures of you in my head
only have me making beds
That we will never lay in.
Yet these movies play in my mind and stay on rewind.
A moment of eye contact is all it took
to f--k up my thought process, entirely.
Even then I saw enough of you,
suffering flashbacks from captured blinks.
Colorblind... As paintbrushes scribed in ink.
Pupils dilate, amazed by your construction zone.
Speed restrictions to aid the building of a vixen.
"God" must have held up traffic trying to make you.
I stare...You glare with those pair of crystals embedded
across a moon brightened sea.
You lie somewhere in the space
between a blink and a tear.
Between captured eyelids lie images of you
that flash in my mind.
I am defenseless to my senses.
This sense of an intenseness.
We have never exchanged words.
I hear your soft vocal cords
though I have never heard your voice.
I can smell you on my nostrils
but we have never stood that close together.
I can taste you on my lips although we've never kissed.
Feel you all over with my hands
although I've never touched you...
Never had a conversation, yet my imagination is
stirred.
Spinning from contemplations of a dream deferred.
Eyes speak to me in a language
only you and I can understand.
So...tell me...Can we play in the dark?

I stare at all that is hidden in plain view.
I am a visionary. Trapped in the gaze of you.
Like having eyes in the back of our heads that never lie.
I wonder what you taste like...
Mmmm. The predictability of the unpredictably.
I want to love you like no one is looking...
Like everyone else is blind.
And, you and I are the only ones who can...
Smell, hear, touch, taste and...
See... your sweat. Soft kisses on damp necks.
Behind closed doors you penetrate my core.
I look. Watch. See...Observe you in the nude.
Beautifully vulnerable and naked.
Connecting spirits from 3rd eye views...
Whatever you give me I will take it.
Let me f--k you like I never met you and
won't be around to judge you after.
Where things don't just happen, but happen just.
For, it's only been 1000 times
since we've never made love.
I can hear the smacking sound,
Skin.   Slapping.   Repetitive.
Motions.
Seeing snapshots of backshots.
With every thrust you come to trust me even more.
Until you let me know it's all in my head.
We don't have to define this.
Never mind this...
Then I wonder why I wonder
only for my thoughts to wander...
Back to you.
I've seen enough of you yet rarely do I see you.
I need you to reject me.

<u>Venom (The Beautiful Poison)</u>

She has lips that taste like venom...
Cause Love is a snake...
Rippling through grass of the unnerved and unsettled.

Removing shoulder straps from her dress...
She lies down in my Kingdom...
Where distance can only be measured by its rulers.

Unbuckling belts from my denim...
I drink venom of its liquid swords.
Slicing me down to paralysis...
The analysis of her silent accord.

Her Queendom...
Ruled by endless walls and many guards.
Which all collapse in my lap...
As I walk barefoot through this yard.

Purity, honesty in my veins... I soon become immune.
Though, Love strikes venom of impending doom...
Biting its victims to open wounds.

With beautiful poison that can cum rushing in waves...
Between her legs lies more venom I crave.
F--k her soft. Make love to her hard.
She never saw me coming.
With Love that challenges guards...
And the sweet taste of a tongue that is numbing.

F--k her hard. Make love to her soft.
Now I see and hear her cumming. Penetrating walls
that are slowly...But, surely crumbling.

<u>Youniverse</u>

I think about you all the time.

I didn't realize how bad it is to crave something

you've never had...

As though you've had it before and many times more.

I know you don't love me the same way I love you.

Truth is, you don't have to.

Truth is, it is impossible to.

Now that I'm awake I have so much trouble

falling back asleep.

I see pictures of you online and my heart jumps.

It's like you're right here next to me.

I can taste your cooking and smell your shea butter.

Having you for thought this morning.

I wrote this verse for you.

The source of all.

<u>?</u>

Can I speak in ideas and possibilities?
While honoring the distance between us?
May I speak in mind of undefined?
Until there is nothing but us between us?
May I greet you at the airport
With the warmth of my vulnerability?
Wave you down with white flags of surrender
Ready to enter into the unknown.
May I remember things you've said
And, hold you to words instead?
May I kiss you with lips of freedom?
And taste the language of your heart's bed?
Can I take your bags? Open your door?
Roll you a joint for elevation?
Ridin' around, vibin' down... to instrumentals...
Around the town 'til we're downtown?
Explore your sounds in surround now?
Taste the restaurants in your down... town?
Can we order to go? To the beach?
Where we can eat in my backseat?
Listen to waves crash and night speak?
Let the breeze cool this flame's heat?
Can I take you home and make you moan?
Bend you over and put you to sleep?
Wake you up with bowls and papers?
Have my breakfast under the sheets?
Can I hold you tight and mold you right?
Reach your body and mind's peak?
Can I cook for you? Can you cook for me?
If I leave will you look for me?
Will you honor my past hungers?
Replenish all that was took from me?
I'll speak in ideas and possibilities
Until there is nothing but us between us.
Create scenarios and fantasies
'til reality is all we've dreamed of.
To be continued...

Lessons

Rain drops stain the window pane.
Your moans stay on my brain.
Your tongue stays on my name...
Or vice versa.
I play my drums to your pain.
Replenishing the youth in your veins.
We light the Sun in Mary Jane
While I strum on your "strangs".
Hydration vibrations until you cum to the rain.
I want lessons in your Love this morning.

Arrive

Queen, I wanna cum for you.
Get lost and run to you.
I want to create rhythms on your body...
Touch the earth and drum for you.
I wanna be fun for you.
Perfect aim. Point guns to you.
Bullets of passion, belts unfastened...
With no intended pun to you.
Like Earth and Sun can do
I want to be the one for you.
I wanna get lost and run to you.
Queen, I wanna come to you.

<u>A Human Experience</u>

I just wanna…
create with you and debate with you.
Go on a date or two and relate to you.
Discuss philosophy while you're naked…
And elated on top of me.

Never mind
birds that flock to me.
I'd rather fly with you like off some weed.
Take you 'round my block like monopoly.
With no possessiveness.
No apostrophes.

But I'm not interested in buying you.
I want to be free and make no sense…
like low highs and lying truths.
Plant seeds. No denying roots.

Allow these trees to grow inside us
like we're the ones providing fruit.
Let's take classes with fails and passes
of all unknowns and perceived truths.

Heal the masses and fill our glasses…
With crashes like alcoholics.
Then question everything to fill our every dream
with strong foundations of love knowledge.

I just wanna
touch you and
clutch you...like it's the last time I will hold you.
And do enough to corrupt you
in a way that this Love can mold you.

Let us
Romanticize
and fantasize
Exchange words that tantalize
the next time we indulge
And can analyze our phantom eyes.

I just wanna
create with you
and debate with you...
Go on a date or two and relate to you.
Discuss philosophy...
But also, while you're fully clothed
and sitting across from me.

War

I hold back.
I hold back from you
From loving you.
From seeing you.
From touching you.
From embracing you.
Pleasing you.
Calling you.
I dare to battle myself.
Courageously.
Like a peaceful warrior.
Breaking through walls that hold knowledge of my
heart.
These battles
Will win me the war.

I dare to love you.
I dare to see you.
To touch you.
Embrace you.
Please you.
I dare to call you.
I dare to battle you.
Courageously.
Like a peaceful warrior
breaking through walls that hold knowledge of your
hearts.
These battles
will win us the war.

Too many battles within ourselves.
Too much confusion between each other.
Our inhibitions versus our intuition.
Growing from trees bearing tastes of fruition.
Fully loving would be diving into
an abyss of the unknown.
With no guarantee of oxygen on these ocean floors,
where new discoveries are made daily.
Loud battles too quiet for us to notice.
Until we butt the multiple heads between us.
We can win the war.
Let us claim the victory alongside each other.

Why?

Because I'm unsure.
Because you don't always make sense to me.
Because I don't always make sense to me.
Because I take responsibility for my trauma
and so do you.
Because I want nothing more than to be close to you
from the other side of the world.
Because I want nothing more than to be close to you
from the other side of the room.
Because I want nothing more than to be close to you
when you're close to me.
Because you don't want kids.
Because I think you'd make a great mother...
Of my children...Maybe.

Because I don't know if I want kids, either.
Because of the thousands of times
I've flown in anticipation of seeing you.
Because I want to be whole yet apart of you.
Because sometimes you just aren't in the mood
and neither am I.
Because I can't read you
due to distance in physical or distance in space.
Because sometimes
I don't understand what I'm doing wrong.
Because I don't want you to change
but I want you to compromise.
Because I want to fill you
with enough Love and passion for your lifetime.
Because I want to overwhelm you with pleasure
until you beg me to stop.
Because I want to overwhelm you with pleasure
until you beg me not to stop.
Because I want access to you
without violating your boundaries.
Because letting you in means I let in us.
Because we are Hip Hop.
Because sharing our passions
for Healing through the Arts
can heal us.
Because I have so much on my plate
but want to fill it with consumptions of your taste.
Along with whatever presumptions we may face.
Because being between your legs
is like when Moses parted the seas.
And going down on you is like if God got on her knees.

I don't know.

Maybe we both seek validation.
Maybe we both seek acceptance.
Maybe we both try to impress.
Maybe our childhoods were too much.
Maybe we can't read our minds.
Maybe we value reciprocity.
Maybe one of us doesn't.
However we react toward one another,
Matters to how we come back to each other.
Because I want you to feel welcome to me
without holding back.
Because, this is all speculation.
Without confirmation, confrontation or validation.
Because I could be wrong.
Because I want to be wrong.
Because I want to be right.
Because I love you...

And the pen is mightier than the sword.

Fall

Too often we are afraid to fall and be caught.
Too often we are made to fly.
So, fall.
Fall like a meteorite.
Fall like October.
Fall like leaves making way for new seasons.
Fall like a skydiver.
Fall like a never-ending roller coaster.
Fall like you have wings.
Fall like comets.
Fall like anchors in the ocean.
Fall like a bungee jumper.
Fall like a glider plane.
Fall like lava from volcanic eruptions.
Fall like Rome.
Fall like an empire to be rebuilt.
Fall like heavy rain that patters away at concrete.
Fall like a bird, spiraling.
Fall like a book from a shelf
That's been waiting to be chosen.
Fall like you slipped down a flight of stairs.
Fall like you've been hit by something or somebody.
Fall like you've fallen and can't get up.
Fall like an angel.
Fall like you tripped over me.
Fall like you will rise again.
Let go and let "God"…
I will catch you.

Court Dates

Like watching a wildfire blazing.
Looking at you is truly amazing.
Looking at you is like stargazing...
The Universe in its old age.
Court dates for our old ways.
We were arsons in old days.
Older now so no judgements.
This here is a closed case.

Forever

Your eyes give an incredible feel.
You're my favorite edible meal.
You heal like you deal in medical fields.
Sending chills thru my skeletal build.
With that love medicine
That's better than it's ever been.
My commander
I'll love you like a veteran
Who's been to war
and has just wanted Love ever since.
I'll put the guns down so my tongue
can run down your spine.
We'll go 'til sun down like we're unbound from time.
You're beautiful. I just wanna be true to you.
Much bigger than intimacy. I want you infinitely.

Miss You

I miss you lying in my bed
With my head between your legs
And, I miss the way your cums sound
When I would tongue you down.
I miss undressing you
addressing what's stressing you.
I miss massaging your back
With you guiding my hands like a map.
I miss being inside you
'til my fingers could feel your arrival
I miss the way you taste
Then wearing your juices on my face.
I miss cooking to feed you
Then kneeling down to please you.
I miss your morning moans
The feel of your morning tone.
I miss you being in your moods
Then kissing away your attitude.
Cause I miss you being near
Your presence. You being here.

I miss f--king you nastily
Being confused while you're mad at me
But I mostly miss greeting you casually
And, knowing this had to be.

<u>But I'm Saying</u>

She moves through the world with no vices.

Has made many sacrifices.

Paid many prices.

Selling Love on tags marked priceless.

Giving breath to the lifeless.

An Egyptian Goddess...She's Isis.

Serving food for thought, adding spices

That'll make you turn off your devices...

And pay attention.

She stands strong thru any crisis.

Word on the street, she's the nicest.

Painting mediums like a psychic.

Hips displaying.

Swaying.

I'm saying...

She's dope.

<u>KEY</u>

I just want to make Love
With no limits. No boundaries.
Ignoring all locks and safes
As if I've found the key.
But first let me break into you
Enter your house not reserved for me.
Steal all your decorated insecurities
Then run off like a burglary.
Leaving you pure. Leaving you bare.
Windows open to ringing alarms.
Open to damage. Open to despair.
But only I can do you harm.
Roofs raised to possibilities
Nothing between floor and ground, now.
Police can respond to these open doors
But I'm the only citizen of your town.
In a neighborhood made by us
No structures crumbling down.
A city for lovers built on trust
With enough foundation to surround.
I just want to make love to you
Like I owe you an apology.
Being gentle on your bodily
Like you're a valued commodity.
No holding back on holding your back
Kiss your neck with lips of honesty.
Go places I've never been before
Like I'm hip to foreign policy.
I want to...Heal your karmic pains.
Speak to your ancestors solemnly.
Make this house of you apart of me
Draw patterns of Sacred Geometry.
Hold you hostage while under the stars
Like we're slaves to Astronomy.

Show you quality over quantity
A new Paradigm. A prodigy.
I'll take your soul to where Goddess be
An astral projection, an odyssey.
Keep you at the center of my universe
Like we've learned from Ptolemy.
Blending our colors with mahogany
Until we are one in autonomy.
Outsiders may seek this colony
But I'll tie you up in monogamy.
I will please you in modesty
Scribble word on your heart's biography.
You'll moan your story so audibly
It'll make this book we write a novelty.
I believe in this Love philosophy.
It sheds all barriers to the bone.
We question things like Socrates
But, Love dwells in the unknown.
I just want to make love to you
With no limits. No boundaries.
'til you look in the mirror and see
It was only you who drowned the key.
I just want to make love to you
With no limits. No Boundaries.
'til you look in the mirror and see
You are much too beautiful for me.

California Dreaming

Last night I dreamed you reunited with your ex
into your family and happily announced your
pregnancy. Today I awoke to this California sunshine,
shedding rays of a reality I find it hard to face.
My chest is on fire. Heavy. I must have let you in.
Thought I was done giving in but Love wins again.
One week from a year of having met you and wanting
you then. How could I let myself fall for someone who
was not available? Crave Love from someone
who is not capable? Maybe because of the visions...

I saw us. Having a family, laughing together, arguing,
making up, dancing and romancing as I moved back to
LA to grow with you. Here in this short amount of time
we have managed to laugh together, make love to each
other 1000 times never, and remind ourselves of what
we value. Courting you and supporting you...I saw us.
Hand in hand. As my wife and lifetime lover. You'd
make a great mother all while in the hands of another.

Truth is, I saw a mirage and chased it to nothing. Now
you're faced with ultimatums and I don't look forward
to waiting. It hurts, burns and makes me wonder if I will
ever find another you. I can't even be mad at her,
though. I would step my game up too if it came
down to losing you. You set up shop in my heart and
made yourself at home. Laid me down in bed to only
dream of you and wake up alone. In hopes that someday
we'll both wake up in a bed together.

But here is where I mistake dreams for reality. Here is
where I step too far ahead, on cliff's edge...not knowing
if I have wings. Here is where I tend to get attached to
alternative facts. Here is where I'm boarding a plane
and leaving from all this California dreaming.

L.A. Nights

Last night I dreamed I slept on the streets of LA.
Woke up downtown to skyscrapers, sunshine in my face.
Didn't know where I was.
But people couldn't see I was sleeping there.
Sat up and looked around.
There were people but they didn't care.
I found it interesting that I found this random mattress.
Near the heart of the city where all the rich
are doing taxes.
Turns out the building I slept behind
was the welfare office.
And other artists I roamed with had slept here often.
But they left me and I had woken up alone.
With no numbers to contact them
and nothing saved in my phone.
The mattress was comfortable
and felt good under the Sun.
Battery low, I finally got in touch with someone
I had been chilling at someone's house.
Apparently, I was homeless.
Went inside the building
and connected with other roamers.
Discussed meditation and Buddhahood, laughed a bit.
Woke up to this empty feeling and now I feel like s--t.
I miss her.

When

You owe me nothing yet you're everything
Come with me. Move on to better things.
A Love enhanced to take a chance
Queen, I'm not afraid of wedding rings.
I want to be in tune with your happiness.
With Love functioning as catalyst.
Fulfilling all of your wants and needs
The one you fight your battles with.
Falling for you has been magical
Based on the actual. Pure factual.
You value dreams that are practical
Yes, Love changes but is absolute.
I just want to kiss you passionately.
Watch you roll a joint then pass it to me
(Cause you don't smoke and that's cool)
I just wanna feel that ass in them jeans.
I'll fuck away your inadequacies
But making love won't matter to me
If the war in you finds no peace
And, I just become a casualty.
Place your skin tone on African thrones
Feeling at home in your cosmic moans
But, getting ahead of Self, apparently
We operate in no guarantees.
I'm standing outside in a thunderstorm
Fully exposed to the lightning.
Aware that safety lies in taking cover,
Struggling to do the right thing.
I stand drenched, knowing the risks.
No obligations from these complications.
I know eventually clouds will clear
And, we can look to the constellations.
A factor for all that comes after.
Seeing you smile, hearing your laughter.
With paint took to blank books
Gives new style to writing chapters.
Things that are broken need maintenance.
We appreciate more what comes in patience.
My mind dwells. But time will tell
Gifting us what is Timeless. What is ancient.
I see longevity beyond seventy.
A legacy transcending heavenly.
Where matters of time become obsolete.
When all we have is Now.
No ifs, ands, buts or maybes.
It's just a matter of when.

Watch

I want to watch you strip.
In high heels.
Sway your stomach and dip your hips
Entice my fingertips. Face close to lips.
I then want to flip you onto your back
Kiss your neck. Get you relaxed.
Run my tongue through all your gaps
And, observe how you react.
I want to get you nice and moist
Til I have no choice,
But to taste you.
With my head between your legs
You moan and beg me to make you...
Cum.
We both know an orgasm awaits you.
I'll watch you explode like it never gets old
Giving muscle spasms as a breakthrough.
Keep your juices on my cheeks
I want to enter you. Go in deep.
Watch you take it 'til eyes meet
And you are flustered, shaken and weak.
Peak reached. You can't speak though.
Choke you out and make you deepthroat.
Watch you leave your body and become Godly...
Now we are something other than people.
You found a locksmith for your keyhole
Opening doors as I turn you over.
Face flat but arch your back.
Watch you take these shots like you're far from sober.
You grab the air as I grab your hair.
You demand that I f--k you right there.
Saying "Just like that" as you scratch.
Now I know being f--ked this good is rare.
Stare. Our eyes meet.
Sweet kisses to sweat on your neck
And all the way down to your feet
But, I restrain you. Not done yet.
Cause I want to watch you ride me.
Make your own rhythm and guide me.
Watch your nipples get hard and lively
Then suck away at them like icees.
Now it's your turn to be inside me....
And, it all began with watching you strip.
In high heels...
So, I hope someday you'll make the trip.

I want to worship you.

The Bliss Continuum

Love is our cosmic ticket.

<u>The Silver Cord</u>

Love is our cosmic ticket.
All aboard this spaceship.

Like a makeshift we use our minds
to travel beyond displacement.
Faced with...
mental attics that tend to dwell in basements.
We transcend these basic spaces...
No longer complacent.
We are the birthers of all creation.
The faces of mankind's races.
We are the basis for time not wasted.
We are psychedelic spacemen.

We travel in mind. We travel in light
Tying these silver string laces.
The aces of love persuasive,
armed with spirit and patience.
We wear time bracelets and stellar rings
Tied to universal silver strings.
In search of all unseen
Hand in hand with my Cosmic Queen.
Vision keen to concentration.
We beam to constellations.
Create serene compilations.
Awakening condensation.

Quantum (Love Mechanics)

Losing weight in outer space is...
food for thought with different taste.

Saying grace at periodic tables...
We embrace.

Taking off from Earth. Taking off your clothes.
The scent of "God" greets my nose.
I then bask in all that cums...and, goes.
You're at the center of my Earth.
Perfect longitude and latitude.
Feeling closer to my creator with you at my equator.

Cause, I draw the line at you...
On this mattress that is sheetless.
We share secrets through telekinesis
Writing Galactic thesis.
Smoking herbs and burning sage
I write us down then turn the page...
Activating optic nerves through the topic of words.
Lying among the medicines our elders have left for us....
We leave and arrive much quicker
Curve your body along the big dipper.

We can't change the past
but we can make a better future
With tantric meditation and the practice of Kama Sutra.
No competition to this composition
Giving you propositions with proper diction.

Glowing human energy field
makes you the perfect energy meal.
Rising above our negatives
with these spacecraft sedatives.
This... trippy psychedelic has high effects on our dialect.
Sacral chakra crystals and 3rd eye stones
spread among the bed.
Candles lit matching the aura colors
on our head of dreads.

Because of you, I know the Universe
Because of the Universe, I know you.

Riding cosmic waves on creative,
innovative arks with native hearts.
Chakras now in alignment
we are freed from material confinements.
Drifting through astral time
and shifting stardust paradigms.

All Systems Go.

*(Silver Cord- When one meditates and transcends to the astral plane,
a thin silver strand ties your eternal being to your physical self.)*

Road Trip

Sunroofs and moonroofs...
Open to the voices of night.
Destination unknown. We own...
These roads free from
Stoplights.
We are on the road to somewhere
With absolutely nowhere to go.
Off road trucks and midnight f--ks...
Detoured roads and deciphered codes.
Endless conversation. Eye contact.
We listen to stars as tires
Roll.
So seductive yet destructive...
This love affair on cruise control.
I take the wheel as you go to feel
Between mobile homes and lane
Dividers.
Campsites and historical landmarks...
No speed limit for these drivers.
"Pull over" You whisper. Softly.
Flashing blinkers road side.
Like a stranger, stranded and in danger
I offer to give you a ride.
I proceed to smother myself in your scent.
Engulfed in every microfiber of your lint.
Shirt removed. Nipples sucked like mints.
All unseen in the shadows of these tints.
Tease me like you need me...
Give me clues. Give me roads. Give me hints.
Let me break you and put you back together.
Screw and repair you like a wrench.
Grant me every inch of your
Skin.
Take me everywhere I've never been.

I move you like mountains and sharp turns,
Show you backseats and rug burns.
Open mics and famous sites...
We pit stop among the nation.
Capture billboards, admire skylines.
Bathroom quickies at gas stations.
This free love that bends
Time.
F--k me with wind's
Mind.
We pit stop among the nation...
Delayed by hotel accommodations.
Lay you down on fresh sheets.
Shed your clothes and flip the
mattress.
Move my tongue along your back.
Guide me through you like an atlas.
Strap up and enter...like I am afraid to surrender to
Love.
Kiss your shoulders then bend you over...
Until your body tells me you're about to
Cum.
So, cum like you're cumming to visit.
Cum like you're meeting me halfway.
Cum like you're cumming over.
So, we can cum to the conclusion
That...
These 24-hour diners in small towns.
Adult stores in the middle of nowhere.
That these back streets and back seats
Entail something far too
Deep.
So, from waterfalls to
Montreal.
At airports in New York.
Watching every sunset and sunrise...

We pass north with passports.
I test your stamina in Canada.
F--king you every time, like I love you.
Making love to you like I hate you.
Foot on gas to accelerate you.
So, on highways and interstates.
Between bridges and underpasses.
Oil changes and city traffic
We can disappear among the masses.
This road trip type love.
We view stars as tires
Roll.
So seductive yet destructive...
This love affair on cruise control.
A journey with no cell phone signals
Away from Facebook and obligations.
Deadlines and avoided questions...
A painfully erotic, passerby type
Obsession.
Temporary lovers and endless moments.
Secrets never once revealed in
Action.
We are bold strangers to the night...
Who return to our lives like it never happened.

Could It Be?

Could it be...
That she is the queen of all moons, suns, stars...
And, the ruler of the seas?
A universal technique...
The power she has over me.
Flowing through me like wind through trees.
A sweet summer breeze.

Emotions swaying like oceans.
Throughout this cycle of life and death.
Keeps me hoping, as my heart remains open.
I yearn to sit and converse.
Explain that she is as natural as the Earth...
And, as pure as the Universe.
I shall put her first,
And make her well aware of her worth.

I do nothing but aim to please.
To have her by my side...Heart at ease.
Shower her with diamonds...pearls...
and all the things greater than these.
For the nature of her alone brings me to my knees.

Could it be... me in the presence of her essence.
Becoming in touch with her past
and at one with her present.
Hips as curvy as the Moon,
when it is bright and crescent.
A feeling so naturally evolving...
Taking me back to adolescence.

Too soon to be serious, yet I find myself curious...
My heart beats vicariously through hers.
Unable to remove her from my thoughts...
Within her innocence I am caught.

And in this position, I find myself in disposition.

A romance so ancient that she rivals the Sun.
I can look to the sky and see the rise of forever.

Her mystic is testing me...
Manifest destiny.
So much to discover...
About this queen... My lover.

<u>BE</u>

Sun closes its eyes.
Moon begins its rise.
You show me how deep love can
BE.
A love everlasting.
A love reborn.
As we lay within these
Sheets.
Open window to the sound
Of night.
Touch. Feel. Cool. Breeze.
Let me
BE
Your comfort.
Your security from this world.
Wrapped in arms.
Our eyes
Connect.
Forget about today.
Worry not about tomorrow.
Bend time to our own clock.
Just let this moment
BE.
No conversation.
Hearts speak.
No sex in physical.
Make love with minds.
Let this
BE
A journey
To somewhere greater.
Where we
BEcome
ONE.

5 Senses

With my 5 senses, no matter the difference...
They are stimulated by you, relieving any tensions.

Seeing you from a distance, I fell in love in an instant.
As seeing love for the first time,
As the first view of light for an infant.
Flashing moonlit crystals scattered on night sea...
I can stare at you for days
with eyes trying to complete your maze.
Hypnotized as your eyes make contact with mine.
They shine, intertwine,
and my sense of sight is forever with you.

And, I am overwhelmed, by my sense of smell.
As you approach me, I am now able to tell...
That your scent is enough to suffocate a room.
With a smell similar to that of spring flowers in bloom,
Or a shower in June. This is the power of your perfume.
Bringing out emotions I never knew existed.
Thoughts being twisted.
Nostrils engulfed in your mystic...
My sense of smell is forever with you.

And, as you whisper gentle words in my ear.
Your voice is the only sound my ears want to hear.
As I listen to sound-waves of us...
Nothing else matters to me.
Whatever that matter may be...
Love communicates in a frequency
That only our bodies can hear.
Your voice provides relaxation with such vibrations.
Now all I hear is temptation. Infatuation.
As my ears absorb this Love education.
My sense of hearing is forever with you.

I need your touch, just as your body needs me.
Hands guided by hunger and your legs feed me.
Making love to you in pitch black.
All I need to do is feel.
Between dark sheets, we are.
All I need to do is feel.
Your brown layer is like a bed of smooth silk.
How is it that something so complex was ever built?
I study your skin's pattern
as though it is a fresh woven quilt.
My sense of touch is forever with you.

Face to face with your thighs,
you leave my buds mesmerized.
You taste like sweet fruit on a warm summer day.
Birds chirping. Love lurking. Seeds bloom from sunrays.
Running my tongue across your navel...
Doing all that I am able.
And, as I play you a tune with my tongue...
Our bodies in rhythm with guitars, pianos, and drums.
Soft melodies and music notes.
I taste the lips they come from.
For my sense of taste is forever with you.

And, with those 5 senses, no matter the difference...
Eternally stimulated by you, relieving all tensions.

<u>Ascian</u>

Touch me, Cosmic Queen.
Find your way beneath my skin.
To discover where our intimacy...
Sheds light on the darkness
Of intricacy.
No night has bearing on your light,
Where the shadow of your love
Reflects upon my very image.
I then lose my train of thought...
Given this one-track mind.
For sounds of freight trains themselves
Cannot even distract me
From our pleasurable indulgences.
Dominance becomes submission,
In that I surrender to your
Security.
Exploring your curves. Quietly.
Intoxicated by scents of your
Purity.
I feel brand new...

Like being reborn on a bed of rose petals.
Exchange of inhales and exhales
To melodic rhythms of affection.

I give.
You take.
We are...
Complimentary soul mates.
From first born creations
We then claim second moons.
The rise and set of an eternal shine,
That will never end too soon.
Like an Ascian
You take me closer to God.
For your love raises me beyond...

Sunlight.

We share never ending moments
Traveling at the many speeds of
Light.

A love that corresponds to the cosmos.
You shield me from all pain.
I am lost among the shadows
In your Divine reflections...
Of perfection.

Cater To You

Long weeks and sore feet.
Overtime and long lines.
Short checks and large debts...
Just come home to me.
Cab fares and bus rides.
Subways and crowded streets.
Briefcases and many faces...
Just come home to me.
Opened door to rose pedals,
Leading into the bathroom.
A bubble bath for your calves...
Playlist of neo-soul and jazz.
I paid the bills, remove your heels.
Put your clothes into the wash.
Just relax. I rub your back...
Clean your body. Dry you off.
Lotion massaged in circular motions.
Dinner is ready on the stove.
Steak and potatoes, the way you like it.
A glass of wine for your mind.
Candle light for the night.
Followed by soft kisses of bliss.
Cuddle and watch your favorite film...
Are you ready for dessert?
Intellectual emulations
Leads to sexual stimulation.
Tell me all about your day...
Then fall in love with me, again.
Cause after long weeks and sore feet...
Overtime and long lines...
Emails and voicemails...
I will cater to you.
Just come home to me.

A Love Universal

Nights no longer sleepless.
Heights no longer reachless.
Sitting here realizing that you are my weakness.
Your depth at its deepest
Has overwhelmed me.
Taken me down to the deepest of oceans
where I drown in my desire
To be with you.
There is a fire in me that burns for you.
A desire in me that yearns for you.
I am unable to comprehend or pretend
that we can only be friends.
The end was the beginning of an end
that is beginning, yet again.
You are my inspiration for everything I write
about the power of love
And, such beauty of a creation that you are by far.
You are the chords when I strum my guitar.
The passion in my rhymes when I spit bars.
These verses bring me back to the surface
When I feel that I have been taken down.
I remember that I am wearing the crown
And, you once a princess of Africa...
Now the queen of my empire.
I am sire.
I picture you in my mind on the throne of our castle.
In a future sweet like apples I see wedding chapels,
Wedding rings and all the beautiful things

a relationship brings.
Poetry nights and open mics.
Flights overseas and making up all night after fights.
This friendship, compassion, and physical connection...
Is a romance with a chance to send
this love to perfection.
I took you for granted and I am lucky you still love me.
Once I believed that you were not for me
And now I am unsure of what I believe.
For years my heart has deceived,
but from you I cannot leave.
I want to be there for you always in all ways on all days
For, in the end it all pays.
I am shouting my love for you,
hearing your name echo down hallways.
So, sitting here looking into your eyes I have
to come to realize
There is no other place in the world I would rather be.
Until the day they bury me I hope you carry me
Beyond the galaxies and stars aligned.
A Love never ending like the skies.
I should be with you. You should be with me
for the rest of our lives.
Ricocheting between Saturn and Mars
In which we are infinitely connected by astrology.
We are astronomically and anatomically
Meant to be.

The Sun (Part 1)

She told me she was used to walking alongside the Sun.
That's why when she touched me
my insides burned so immensely.
"Fear not the fire,
Nor the flames." She said.
"My love is thermodynamic.
Join me in the Sun".

Stay

I expect that you will never lie
Unless it is next to me.
I expect that you will never cry
Unless they're tears of ecstasy.
A new found recipe
You're food for the soul.
Stay and move me with your mind...
Telepathy.

Wings

My love, let us walk to the edge of uncertainty...
For only the ego fears the unknown.
Empty of fear and full of you...
We jump.
What did I tell you?
Turns out we have wings.

Moon Rising

I want to rise with you
Like...
Cream rising to the top of mental morning mugs.
You represent every edge of my thinking
Sipping and drinking...
I want to rise with you.
Like the sun appears to do
when the Earth turns to greet it
Creating shadows, shedding light on all
we've both defeated.
I want to rise with you in evolution,
via revolutions around the Sun.
As night arrives and mystic dew of a new day comes.
I want to rise with you every morning.
Forming...
Space between our toes and the rough concrete.
I want to rise with you in upward motion...
Onward and beyond.
Getting lost in the waves of cosmic oceans.
Shattering conflicts under elevated aggressions.
I want to rise with you to levels of only God's discretion.
Beyond weapons of mass destruction,
we rise above the mass's construction.
I want to rise again with you...like Lazarus.
I want to rise with you like we have died
for each other's sins.
Having since resurrected the outs of each other's ins.
As molecules and particles show me the heart of you
from start of you...
Queen, all apart of me is a part of you.
Rising signs of universalism,
Making love to universal rhythm.
Building passionate spaceships, using passionate tactics.
Mindless and mindful... Curving spineless chiropractic.
We share love among this Milky Way galactic.
Rising through nebulas and wormholes
Where empty souls turn whole.
We let this sage burn slow...Then we go.
I want to rise with you in strength
Like tidal waves and roses in bloom.
Together we rise in growing light...
Like waxing gibbous moons.

Revival

I lie on her stomach and kiss her back.

As the first, second and third act

She is Love's playwright. My sunshine in daylight.

Wrap her in towels of my letters and vowels.

From the womb to the tomb she'll be beautiful.

Like moon to sun, and cycles rebirthed in funerals.

I don't have very many "beautiful' s" left.

I breathe and don't feel they are suitable breaths.

As her heat radiates this bullet proof vest

It shows that all things blossom and die the most

beautiful deaths.

And, this Love was the first step

Toward reviving the beats in my

chest.

Merkaba

Tattooing Mandalas on our spirits.

Transcendental meditation leads to this awakening.

Extraterrestrial hobbies bring life to celestial bodies.

I keep this in mind while undressing your Godly.

Planting Love flavored seeds in the root of our lives.

Gaining soul nutrients from the fruit of the skies.

I move my hands along your face

and down over your waist.

Shedding excess weight like we're in outer space.

Chills sent down this astronaut spine.

Your interstellar debris leaves me temporarily blind.

So, I'm speaking to you through spirit.

Beyond the vacuum of space, you'll hear it.

Here we communicate through the Merkaba...

Beings on mountains to beings on solar wings.

Cause, this is Love in the times of science.

This is Love.

This is Love.

Light-Year

Kiss her like I miss her.
Touch her like I clutch her.
Move her like I soothe her.
Like Pink Floyd
it is the dark side of the Moon we avoid.
Freudian slips into her divinity.
I'm high on her serenity.
To infinity and beyond...
Buzzing me light years over radio waves
and mental peaks.
She cooks up nebulas for me with no clothes on.
Rolling us joints while we just hang out
and write together.
I see now that I must learn not to question these things
Giving way to hopeless romance and falsified dreams.
Charged crimes of occupying my mind
with no evidence...
She's more important to my world than the president.
My dreams keep me moving
but her love keeps grounded.
If I can't be your homie-lover-friend
can I be your only lover then?
An entirely new breed of woman,
with soul trapped and now freed.
Rest assured you're the best for sure.
I don't think she believes me when I say
her entire being intrigues me.
Filling the back of my eyelids with fantasies of her.
Tantalized by her eyes.
Having memorized each detail they entail
Like masterpieces painted for the mind's eye.
I don't want to write this poem anymore.
I just wanna be with you.
I just wanna see you through
To infinity and beyond.

Thinking

I'm thinking of roses that grow from concrete.
Thinking of Hip Hop events & Mobb Deep
Thinking I love the taste
Of love and hate
Dubs and tapes.
Thinking of rhythms and all "isms"
We've created.
I'm elated... thinking of sounds and towns (I've never
been to)
Crowns and thrones.
I'm thinking of grounding homes
In our heads and hearts.
I'm thinking we led the start
Of something that is transcending
Man's ending.
Thinking of the end of time
Thinking of pens and rhyme
Spending time (over our)
Sins and crimes
I'm thinking of troubled pasts and doubled math's of
down under.
Struggled laughs of wonder
When healing.
I'm thinking of healing this. Dealing with
Anything.
Thinking of forgiveness and growth.
Lyrics and ropes.
Thinking of hanging onto this hope.
Headboards banging
Thoughts rearranging to vulnerability and love agility.
Above tranquility
I'm thinking of depths and highs
Steps to climb.
Breasts and thighs.

Thinking to step aside and let spirit talk.
Thinking spirit can talk so spirit can walk
With thoughts in mental vaults
Outlined into chalk (body).
I'm thinking of emotions and pleasure.
Notes and measures.
Oceans and treasures
Buried deep in her legs
Secrets she keeps in her head
While thinking of me.
I'm thinking of we.
Thinking of she.
Thinking of all this can be.
I'm thinking of music and soul.
The rubrics of gold.
Coolant to cold
Instead of heat.
Truth be told
In light of the streets
we walk.
I'm thinking of tires and desires
Of cars and sky blanketed stars.
Rental cars, pool tables & bars.
While driving and smiling.
Hand in hand on candid cams.
Finding us in stranded lands.
I am a fan.
Thinking of highs and lows.
Eyes and toes.
Fingers and teeth.
Cell phone ringers and beats.
Thinking of lips and hips.
Curved dips and fluidity drips

On her body.
Thinking of hobbies and hotel lobbies.
I'm thinking I'll "prolly"
Keep thinking about thinking.
Keep drinking her on this thinking.
Sipping and tipping at this bar.
Where she serves
Words, verbs and herbs.
Thinking of patience and maintenance
Thinking of waiting like a waitress.
Serving food for hearts
When she's ready to start
Her order.
Thinking of different positions
With no restrictions.
Rhymes and beats.
Finders, keeps.
Sex vocals and local eats.
I'm thinking of everything.
Thinking of nothing.
Thinking of touching...
You.

I'm thinking of you.

Mountain (Vegas)

The mountains in Las Vegas still have a lot to say.
They speak to me in confidence
when no one is listening.
As the sun sets behind them
I can hear them whispering.
Speaking through the many layers of my conditionings.
I'd travel along their gravels...
In the shadows of my battles...
As those mountains steepened, I kept on ascending.
As the water deepened, I learned the value in
swimming.
Like I had to earn my right to breathe with less oxygen.

As the dry ached the feet of mental moccasins...
I am convinced I was in love with you
well before we met.
Well before this city of sin...
Well before we had skin...
Well before time or the existence of mind.
Well before "before"...
When we were one with all that is.
Before mountains formed and the Sun was all that was.
My love for you had no beginning and no end...
Just as dessert trails with a mirage at every bend.

You took me hand in hand,
walking this sacred mountainous land...
Of climbing elevations and meditations.
The mountains would say hi
and my mouth would be dry
but you hydrated me like vapors from the sky.
So, the mountains in Las Vegas still have a lot to say.
They speak to me in confidence
when no one is listening.
As the sun sets behind them
I can hear them whispering.
Speaking for the many layers of Love's conditioning.

The Healing Continuum

I published a book in her name.

<u>Bookshelf</u>

I published a book in her name.

But my words crumbled.

Falling victim to her attempted edits.

Blank pages became filled...

With red inked letters.

Permanently.

From an inevitable impermanence.

I stopped writing.

She stopped reading...

My precious flaws.

I am now just another book on her shelf

Filled with chapters she was unable to decipher

Among pages that once cut our fingertips...

Until we no longer touched.

I just hope she'll always love me...

Though she never read me cover to cover.

Razorblade Suitcase

I carry this suitcase full of razor blades.
Light and darkness have come together...
Emitting this gray colored shade.
To move on, I am too afraid.
Scanning the streets for First Aid.
Desperately. Courageously.
Yet all signs of help just fade.
I am trying to escape this mess we made.
This was our creation. Our escapade.
This is the type of game that has already been played.
Now, I run... dismayed.
Her? Confused. Betrayed.

I'm alone...
But her baggage I still carry in my hands...
I open it. Blades slash my skin.
Again, she wins.
She was my overdosing drug.
And this suitcase holds the ingredients...
Composed of all we were made of.

Pain...
Is all this suitcase contains.
It is written all over our names
Along with shame and disdain.
I stand here in this rain,
Attempting to hold my head up high...
But I am too red with pride to admit I am dead inside.
Baggage much too hard to just set aside.

So, I can't help but reach inside.
Cut.

We built this then killed this.
I look behind me and try to hide.
Holding on to my past...
Though, I know that is where pain resides.

She has become an anomaly
To which I have to break free.

But this pain hurts so good.
I can't, but I should.

This razorblade suitcase...
Empty with so much of our happiness.
So, I must fight the urge to reach in and feel.
I search for strength to keep moving
Since all wounds eventually heal
And time eventually kills the urge to look back.
I need to feel. I need to feel...
The lies, fights, and distrust.
Breathing slowly, I tell myself...
I won't miss much.
Not wanting to let her go but I need to let her know.
I have lost too much blood...
And can no longer hold this weight.

The hypocrisy of lust.
This monstrosity of cuts.
Are definitive...
Representative...
Of the philosophy of us.
I gather strength
To clean the infections from these wounds.
Give them air
Give them space
Give them room.
I know someday I will see her again.
Maybe soon.
And I'll be healed with an open heart.
I will be immune.

Black

Moments of love pass through my mind

As I stare in the mirror.

Seeing clearer

As I swallow my pride

And, accept inside

There is no longer a you and I.

"You" and "I"...

Two words once lived by...

Shared beautiful times with a beautiful mind.

A burning flame in your heart is now cold and blue.

Reminisce on these feelings...

Both old and new.

I told the truth

When I said you just happened to be

The best thing that ever happened to me.

What we thought was good, was only blackened

beneath.

She Asked Me...

She asked me to write her a poem.
And, all the norms surrounding love
in its purest form cannot deny the fact
that this
Is a bad storm.
The rain is pounding and the wind is up-rooting trees.
This isn't a sweet summer breeze, like my other poems.
I'm clinging to a branch and holding on...
To nothing.
Cause clearly, we don't get along
and I'm the one that's always wrong.
She's the lyric to every sad song I've ever written.
Many a times I've told her good riddance.
Told myself to stay strong... but I didn't.
The pain no matter how excruciating, I've still forgiven.
"Love is stronger than pride." – Sade
I know I never stepped up the plate.
But, I'm not even sure she wanted to pitch to me.
How do you say "I'm not over you" when such words
are long overdue?
Laced with giant meanings that remain hidden
in plain view.
Out of mind when out of sight...

I hope her new Love is treating her

right. Don't want to come between

that... (yeah I don't really mean that.)

We aren't right for each other...We've both seen that.

And in that extreme fact I refuse to believe that.

Because I still miss when she'd relax and lay flat...

And just before her climax she'd freeze...

squeeze...and, arch her back.

I miss her moans... And, sometimes I think about that.

Though, the bad times were a fist full,

other times were blissful.

When I see her face I'd forget about all past issues.

Maybe we'll work out our differences

and she'll come to her senses.

We reside on different sides...

Separated by invisible fences.

So close to a distant love by only inches.

The word beautiful simply does not describe her.

I still find her laid out over my thoughts

like a fresh cut fade.

In this odd position, she still has no competition.

I miss her.

I even miss the arguments. Though, they only signified...

Dignified our relationship.

Still we sailed out and set sea on that relations ship.

And, she was the only one I had relations with.

Now I miss her kiss, her lips... and I hate this s--t.

Even after she left,

I could still smell her in my sheets...

Could still taste her when I'd eat.

I could still feel her heart beat.

The pain caused was not intentional.

The breakup was unpreventable.

But, to this day I remain sensual.

Cause my love for her is unconditional...

And, such a love is multi-dimensional.

, she asked me to write her a poem.

And, she doesn't know she crosses my mind

every time I wake up.

Sometimes, late at night, I just wait up...

Trying to make sense of it all.

I don't know what the future holds.

I don't know where we may go.

But I hope one day we won't be so sensitive

or argumentative.

Maybe we both need to time on our own to grow.

But only time will come to show.

Only time.

When It Rains It Pours

The storm has arrived.

You are not as you once seemed.

I saw the clouds and smelt the rain.

But didn't think it would come.

Yet, the inevitable has happened...

Lightning strikes and I am wet.

Soaked. Drenched. Hurt...

In never ending downpour.

Tears drip down my cheeks

Blending in with drops of rain.

Lightning never strikes the same place twice...

Yet, hearts seek shelter under trees.

Rumbles of thunder heard from within.

I grab ahold of something in this wind.

They say when it rains it pours.

But you never rain. You just pour.

Magnet

Northern bound...
I am.
Since we no longer meet...
Halfway.
Equators erased
From planets we tilted...
To altered rotations.
Causing our waters to rise...
Mountains to fall...
And, many suns to
Scorch hearts.
Every moon being stripped of
the strength that once held us
together.
I lose blood
From being drawn to...
Your need for my universe's
iron.
But hearts of steel
do not attract
On any plane of this...
Ecliptic.
I yearn for overwhelming force...
Like your love letters
Posted on my refrigerator.
But you only pull me in close enough
For comfort.
Then you flip and...
Repel.

Your Seasons

I no longer feel for you
And, you're asking for reasons.
I don't know how else to explain
Other than to tell you about your seasons.
First came spring
And, flowers began to grow.
Just like our love
And, the wind softly blows.
We get a few showers
But they quickly pass through.
Then summer arrives.
And there's whole new you.
You begin to sweat me
Just like the Sun.
It storms a lot more now
So, I stay inside 'til you're done.
Here comes autumn
And leaves start to fall.
Just like our Love
And I don't understand it at all.
Then it begins to snow.
I guess winter has come.
When I try and touch you
You're cold, my fingers go numb.
It's so brisk out now
And you won't let me back inside.
I slip and fall on your ice
And it damages my pride.
I want to go somewhere
That it is spring all year.
I can't handle your different seasons
So I must leave here.

This Guitar

This guitar calls out my anger.
This guitar calls out my plea.
You bought this guitar for me.
So, you'd probably disagree.
Carefully, I study the chords.
To our love, this guitar is tuned.
The clock strikes noon.
I write lyrics to see you soon.
This guitar is you and I.
I play with rhythm to the drum.
Wondering what time you will come.
Impatience grows as I strum.
This guitar contains melodies.
I sit and strum this six-string.
I try to think of a song to sing
About the love you said you'd bring.
Run fingers over body and neck.
This time, I am so over the top.
I keep playing, I can't stop.
I strum so hard the strings pop.
This guitar is our love.
At a picture of us, I stare.
I swing my guitar into the air.
It crashes down, pieces everywhere.
This guitar symbolized us.
It sounded sweet ballads and noise.
Once so elegant and poise.
Now this guitar is destroyed.

The Mist

A being of powerful eloquence.
I was once lost in your benevolence.
With a design so pure of nature
You should be among the table of elements.
I am highly convinced
you are none other than heaven sent.
But, in matters of intelligence
I know what I feel is irrelevant.
You've been selfless...
I've been selfish.
Opposites attract, yet here I stand helpless.
And I have felt this
For a long time. Figuring I had dealt with...
My insecurities.
Yet you have only witnessed acts of foolery...
Immaturity...
And now I doubt my purity.
For I have to be better for me
Before I can be better for you.
My internal evolution...
This revolution will not be televised.
Neither can it be digitized or criticized
By you.
You hate that I cannot legitimize our truth...
But my heart still grows intellectually
And, Love deserves the best of me.
Now, in this mist things have only gotten blurry.
I cannot let you go without worry
And, you cannot force me to hurry.

Instead of walking this path as one unit...
We just f--ked up a situation,
Brought chaos into patience.
So, I can't blame you abandoning station

Words are the resolution to this conflict...
I just haven't been able to speak.
You have not gotten what you requested
And, your stomach can no longer digest it.
I'd do away with your heart's contusions...
But I am so into me I can see why you feel neglected.
Until I do this for me, we can't be
what you want us to be.
I know it hurts you just as much as it hurts me.
I can only promise you one day
That this will all be behind us.
That WE will still find US...
Somewhere in this mist.
You have no choice but to leave and protect yourself
While I attempt to correct myself...
But there is nothing in the world
that hurts more than this.

I thought I was ready.
I'm sorry.

The Bronx Is Burning

I once heard that monogamy rhymes with monotony.
Maybe that's why I always end up in jail
when I play monopoly.
Never been good at playing games,
I'd rather lie next to you and give you my name...
But there is no use in trying to move mountains
if you live in the plains.
In our effort to shed the pain we left footprints on the
Moon's terrain...
But there is no use in shooting for the Sun
if you have no aim.
So today, I walk through the Bronx with no sign of you.
Like a contract missing an endorsement...
I'm an army of one without reinforcement.
We managed to sign on dotted lines with no name...
Between Yankee games and vacation planes
I never believed we'd be in pain.
Let it be known I never meant to implement
such a predicament.
When I boarded those flights out of LaGuardia
my skin was covered in your fingerprints...
What good is an age-old tree if it has no foundation?
No roots?
When we opened our minds to the impossible
it was then that we found the truth.
That low key you know me better
than anyone else ever could.
Now I can't come to the Bronx and to deny you've
become a part of me.
I remember the sounds of Salsa
blasting from many stereo speakers.
Seeing high schoolers on the 4-train
wearing only the freshest sneakers.
Getting cursed out in Spanish
and needing you as my translator.
Homeless men standing outside a bank

asking each passerby for favors.
Listening to cab horns and fire trucks
roll by on our 4th story apartment.
Being reminded of the beginning.
We went from loving hard to loving heartless.
I'll never forget the sushi restaurants,
City Island, and Orchard Beach...
Groceries from Food Bizarre in our fridge
and crossing the George Washington bridge.
I'll never forget waking up those mornings
and seeing Jupiter set, east of the fire escape.
Taking the 6 bus out to your mom's house
around the corner from where Hip Hop was born.
Counting the stars and catching eclipses...
Our love seemed to arrive in shipments.
You prepared special meals for my fitness...
We had a simple kind of life.
Made of fabric among the Sun...
Everybody around us believed you were the one.
So, when I see NY Timberland boots,
it only brings about remembrance of you.
Seeing signs for the Bronx Zoo while riding in cabs
along Kingsbridge Avenue.
New York Yankee logos on hats
and those huge D train rats.
You sat with me at Bronx Lebanon for hours
waiting to see a doctor.
And on any days of Boredom
we'd just hop on the 41 and ride to Fordham.
We'd catch movies on Saturdays,
after doing laundry together around the corner.
Visiting the Bronx Museum of the Arts
and you showing me Van Cortlandt Park.
You'd even hold my hand when the crowds
and subway tunnels made me anxious.
Hence why I struggle letting go.
Hence you having been my closest acquaintance.
Then like a mirror to broken glass

you went from a cool blue to flaming red.
Only those with hearts which never bled
would believe this romance is dead.
Being snowed in together
and Dominican parades canceled due to rain.
Here in the Bronx prices stayed the same,
but our currency has appeared to change.
It is true that there is no great love
where there was no great passion.
We couldn't travel down this road without crashin'.
We just moved too fast.
I peeled your heart away like petals
and left your stomach unsettled.
Maybe one day you'll forgive me when you see
I only loved you the best way I could.
You blessed my life for a reason
and I'm glad to still be breathing.
There have been times that from all the bleeding...
I thought that hurting you would kill me.
Having to leave you behind
was like telling the Sun not to shine.
So I watch sunrays on Sundays,
reminiscing on the times.
If monogamy rhymes with monotony
then I don't want to play monopoly.
Against the odds we loved so freely
and wrote it on walls like Bronx graffiti.
If the time once was taken to rebuild a borough
that appeared long gone...
I find hope in what I destroyed,
having set fire to a structure so strong.
We took the pain the max.
Took on flames then collapsed.
But we had to destroy to rebuild...
And, the Bronx is still burning.

Bullets

I miss you like bullets
That hit walls in my aim to please.
Armed with these...
I shoot.
Penetrating your skin.
Now I just miss you.
And, I miss you.
Empty lips to empty clips.

Brake Dance

We move too fast so we brake
Dance.
Bending and twirling.
Throwing bodies to the rhythm of touch.
She breaks
Hearts.
Then brake
Dances.
Hip Hop rhythm of screeching tires.
Breaking backs.
Breaking bones.
We dance
With no seatbelts.

<u>Chess</u>

Pawn me.

Send me out on the frontline...

Where sacrifices made begin to fade.

"L" shapes stand for "Love"

Among the journey of Knights...

You just kill your opponents, refusing to keep score.

Movements are limited so we strategize.

"Checkmate". Check your mate. We move to satisfy.

Making "exes" out of Bishops

No rules in your book.

We're left and right... Up and down...

King de-castled like a Rook.

You win the battles. You win the war.

That's what your love of chess is for.

Bring out the Queen at crunch time...

For I'm the Pawn on frontlines.

You'd murder your Queen to corner a King.

These are the games you play.

Left out in the open...

We both lose.

Music

You are a secret untold.
A song no one has ever heard.
Until you, this guitar sat like an old wall clock.
Hollow and enriched of dust...
Empty and lacking of trust.
I let go and collapsed into you...
Bettering my overall performance.
Your body would relax in my arms
As I gently kissed your neck.
You would moan to pleasures of my touch.
Bring melodies to my fingertips.
Under the spell of your eargasms
I was compelled to compose more notes.
But as soon as this song was written

Our strings fell out of tune.

For quarters of time on our staff

Were at a rhythm not meant for speed.
Now off beat with no song to sing...
These six strings no longer ring...
And all between now means...
Nothing.
I used to never miss a beat.
I'll still sing these songs forever.
For, I have faith in the longevity
Of each measure.

Blame it on the Sun

Today I had to looked in the eyes of a Goddess...
And was finally honest.
That after all this time it's important to say...
I may go astray.
Nothing just happens. Things happen just...
We've been here lifetimes upon lifetimes.
If monogamy is what you need, I get it.
I'm running out of lifelines.
She says she only wants to be with me.
I respond that I can't just love one woman.
But everything I do is for her...
Just like she'd prefer.
I can't be confined...
But it's important that I speak
on the grounds of reassurance.
I seek your trust and this is my truth...
Am I good enough for you?
They put on disguise, see only their eyes...
Yet I am one unmasked.
You've been through masquerades
upon masquerades of lies
In attempts to make love last.
So, I blame the Sun signs.
This is flawed astrology...
Eye owe you an apology.
Can't tell planets from stars
So meet me halfway...
I just want you to stay.

R.E.M.

They say in a dream anything goes.

We can think something and it will instantly manifest.

We have phone conversations that never happen...

Exchange words that are never said...

Share romance like there is only us...

And sit on each other's minds like we belong.

Like a selfish child holding tightly

onto the sweet taste of

heart shaped lolli pops...

We touch like there's no tomorrow...

And, see the world like we're on Venus.

We feel no guilt for what is meant to be...

Say hello to goodbyes.

For in a dream anything goes...

Even lies.

<u>Corona</u>

I think of her in circles

Like sunrise to sunset.

My planets reflect her shine

Like drummer to drum set.

Goddess of light. Maker of Venus.

I'm a moon that is crescent.

I rise and fall with her.

Intoxicating depressant.

Falling stars and comet impacts

Leave me with beautiful craters.

Rising tides and gravity turns

From her shifts of my equator.

So, I think of her in circles

Like sunrise to sunset.

Now my planets reflect her darkness

Like drummer to drum set.

Unstable Atmosphere

It's raining this mourning.
I guess it was going to begin storming.
Before I awoke to this pain
with little to no warning.
It is lightening and I can feel
the drops pouring.
Pounding at my heart well before clouds
were even forming.

Dead End

I saw the signs.
Had enough time
And, turned down this road, anyway.
Full of potholes and barriers,
I'm swerving.
Braking fast for my
Freedom.
U-Turning while you're burning
My rubber.
Acceleration to liberation from
Dead ends for lovers.
Gotta find another way home to me.

The Possibilities in Impossibilities

I believe in the possibilities in impossibilities.
This dark side of the Moon type love.
Where wolves gather and hearts shatter
And, all that matters after is us.
This is a love neither of us
have come to master and trust.
Somewhere in between this laughter and lust...
we exist in fear.
This is a book where reading every chapter is a must.
But you've started another book
while this one has yet to be written...
Like a seer who was blind, you spoke and I listened.
Blink...
Cause following your voice erased my fears.
Vocal tone spoken from your throne and moans that
turned seconds to years.
Bending and breaking at your every call.
One look at you and I'd seen it all.
Given our chemistry you finished me,
yet I could touch you endlessly.
You entered my life from afar,
like an angel giving birth to stars.
With nothing but a dream and our guitars
we set ship and left Earth for Mars.
But there are lessons in such obsessions and it appears
I've failed the final test.
For I lay bruised. Broken. Battered.
All bent up in a spinal mess.

A hidden, forbidden love
like kids playing in rain under a storm.
I ignored the thunder yet now I wonder
why it appears that pain is the norm.
We danced in amusement parks and searched the lost
and found for our minds.
Too busy circling around the signs
That this would die a thousand times.
We dreamed of camping trips and seaplanes...
Canoes and rough terrains.
We spoke of secrets that we'd keep
and played emotional hide and seek.
The way your body curved to my lips
I was so sure you were made just for me.
It was as though I'd discovered a precious gem
no one else was meant to see.
But if time is a waste of my time
then heart is a waste of reasonable mind.
For, I had my qualms about it
yet I was always calm without it.
Singing lullabies like astronauts,
we sat and played tunes for the moon.
So, I gathered brooms and swept the darkness
under rugs of our rose painted room.

Blink...
Cause following your voice erased my fears.
Now your hips speak in a language
I only fail to comprehend.
Lips explain like drips of red wine.

A Love that died like brick to dead vines.
Worshipping you, I parted seas in prayer
like toasting bread to wine.
Food for thought, I fed your mind.
Shit I was scared, too. I was unprepared for you...
Though we found balance within our talents.
We drank out of half empty glasses
and chipped away at broken bowls.
We even managed to fill Love's fridge
with empty bottles and open lids.
You don't believe in sequels or trilogies...
You create your own impossibilities...
Still, it was hard to believe
when you actually showed
you're no longer feeling me.
So, your tunnel visioned direction
now reflects upon my imperfections.
And, to think... I once howled at moons
and sang to satellites at your discretion.
I will always believe
in the possibilities of impossibilities.
I just understand there is no hope here
for those who push away in order to cope here.
After tasting your wine,
my will to love died a little every time.
I've now turned from those lips that once parted seas
but only sank ships in mine.

<u>Words</u>

You once told me you'll never come back
to a professional wordsmith.
For you now believe I can create a
tangling web of lies with my gift.
Yet here I stand on many stages,
flipping throughout the many pages
Of my dictionary...
Just trying to find the words.
That's a first. It appears my gift has become a curse.
I've been forced to silence my tongue
and ignore the vibrant of drums.
Like writing songs without verse,
without bridge, without chorus.
I search for words in a thesaurus
to find my way out of this forest.
We were two wanderers
dancing rhythms to our metronome.
Yet, this black on black monochrome
now reflects in monotone.
...We traveled together and now we travel alone.
Not sure how we got here
since you stopped answering your phone.
What exactly did I do wrong?
Was it telling the truth...
about how you never got to raise my daughters
but have raised plenty of my Suns?
I'm not trying to charm you; I'm just saying what I feel.
Yet, it seems I've made it hard for you
to tell when a poet is being real.
It's as though I stood before Love's judge
on an indictment of infidelity...
With proceeds of bail arraignments

due to a failed engagement.
I understand that for us to heal
it is better that we don't speak.
We need not know nuclear fusion
to feel the intensity of this heat.
I'm speechless, having been forced to keep this
A secret.
Though I awake every morning in bliss
having dreamed of your goodnight kiss.
I lay here in bed wrapped so tightly
in my insecurities and flaws.
I rise and shine with eyes so blind...
Searching for your voice of universal law.
I miss when you'd talk to me
and tell you're about to cum.
Whisper sweet nothings to me
and let the words roll off your tongue.
Now there are scratches on my heart
to match the ones you left on my back.
It is almost intentional how Love can be so medicinal.
I see the sounds and hear the light...
I touch the air and breathe the texture...
I want you to know for all you've given me,
I never felt you imprisoned me.
If we are truly soul mates
then it is not up to us to control fate...
I just find it odd that our hearts still beat
for something you claim is dead.
Now, whispers of a violent silence
creep along these walls in the dark.
A quiet riot of a thousand candles
are burning in my heart.
You don't say. No, you really don't say.
I need something to go on here

but you've left me with nothing.
Tell me more...
Please, just speak to me.
I used to kiss you like I was trying to get to your heart
and the only way to it was through your mouth.
The shadow of your words reflects upon my very image.
I have yet to find another pair of
lips that they mimic.
Like moon to sun and sky to ground,
I look up and then down.
Like sight to sound and noun to verbs,
I look back on us and address the words.
Having chosen to ignore this,
we are the elephant in the room.
But if we are not willing to dance
then never mind the tunes.
A Love like ours contains vocab
that unlocks secrets of the wind.
But I'll swallow my words and bite my tongue,
then never speak on this again.
I found our voice but lost our words.
Found the words but lost our voice...
With the pain of talk you'll forever take
what I say with a grain of salt.
I won't speak on this connection
and how the heat is too high.
Cause if you don't have s--t else to say, neither do I.
I see now that falling trees go unheard in this forest.
I believe the grass is greener on both sides.
It's the trees no one pays attention to.

The Learning Continuum

When pain is the only emotion felt...

Forgiveness

When pain is the only emotion felt...
Blinding you from all else.
Breaking you down and clouding your thoughts...
The pen helps.
Yet, staring at these blank pages.
I must consider the wages dealt.
She deserves happiness
And is happy...
With a heart now occupied by someone else.
Unable to move to the news.
No motivation, for I grasp too tightly
All I should let go of...
A now buried love.
Only to be haunted by nightmares
Where she is there and I am confronted...
Forced to awaken alone and bare.

By letting her go I did US a favor.
We used to wake the neighbors.
Not always with love making
Sometimes with anger.
Where I would argue just to argue.
There she goes with no regrets
Moving forward without our past.
Here I am with a suitcase full of razorblades
Hurting myself over what could not last.
When she thinks of me, I hope it is only good
thoughts. That one day we will talk
And be able to laugh about yesterday.
I know it's okay
To miss waking up to her every
day. Looking into those brown eyes

Full of hope and hopelessness...
Wanting to make this work.

Unable to face her...
I left.
Maybe it is better that we not communicate.

So stubborn...
I fight the urge to call
Because I know it is too late.
I just want to hear her voice,
Have her tell me she is happy. Content.
She met my past, not what I am becoming.
Something I regret but could not prevent.
It happened for a reason
I know I must let this go.
Evolving minds and hearts in conflict.
How did we get so low?
Actions easier said than done.
We were one, times were fun...
Given the chance I would fix this, entirely.
But it's done.

So when pain is the only emotion felt
The pen helps.
And, it hurts...

I just hope she forgives me
Since I couldn't forgive
myself.

Agree to Disagree

I don't understand you sometimes.
Cause even through the fun times
we always end up confined
To your insecurities.
I'm sure you'll be in dismay if I ever went astray
but I shouldn't have to reassure you
that I won't every day.
You say actions speak louder than words.
So, I reiterate this through to communicate it to you.
Yet, somewhere in between our communication
we get lost in word translation
And it only leads to prolonged days and sleepless nights.
You project. I deflect.
I project. You deflect.
No one wants to take responsibility for their actions
and give respect.
So, do I start packing or do I keep acting
like it's just another fight?
Or do I settle my pride and apologize
since I'm always right?
We're always too busy proving our points
so no one ever listens.
You always feel like I'm too critical of your decisions,
but I...
Clearly see more in you than you see in yourself.
So, can we just agree to disagree for a change?
You say I'm too defensive
and I think you're too sensitive.
I say you're too needy, you think I'm just self-absorbed.
But we cannot afford to lose what we have.
Between the laughs and heartfelt jabs,

we are rich with vitality.
I fall in love with you again every time we fight.
Behind it I am reminded
that I want to lay with you every night.
I may need a break from you every now and then
but that's alright
For you are the very definition of what
it means to live a dream.
We value the same things so why can't we compromise?
Constantly we speak of tools we have yet to utilize.
Every now and then when I look into those eyes
I admire our togetherness and willingness
to get through this.
So, can we agree to disagree?
I believe in a love that surpasses breasts and asses.
What we have transcends the masses idea
of all that is romantic.
I admire your little antics
and though sometimes I make you frantic
My love for you is scribed, solidified...
As though it was written in Sanskrit:
"Tat Tvam Asi".
There will always be those who say
they will but they won't.
Those who say they love you but they don't.
Through it all you've inspired me
to love in spite of this truth.
You always find ways to return me
to the innocence of my youth.
So why do I have to be careful who I compliment?
Even if it's a woman on another continent
You always allow it to chip away at your confidence.
If only you were aware that I awake to you

every morning in astonishment
Would you cease to have so much incompetence
on your consciousness?
As long as we are free to love beneath our maker
I will continue to give you the best that I've got...
Anita Baker.
Even if I am left to pick up the pieces in
the darkness of these hardships,
Please trust and believe I will always
put us back together.
I don't know how I became this brainless,
painless, shameless in that I hang this
vanquish picture of us on my soul.
But I blame this and frame this
on the stainless "steal" of my
heart.
For happiness is not available
without some disagreements.
I've been knocked down
and did not believe I could get up.
I've been told to pack my s--t up and keep it moving.
And here you came...close to me,
where you were always supposed to be.
So, why are we arguing with me?
Can't we just agree to disagree?!?

<u>The Poem You Always Wanted</u>

My Downelink profile is now closed.
Signifying the end of an era I suppose
Was the source of our highs and lows.
This is all so bittersweet.
Somewhere in between
where "moving on" and "bitter" meet...
We now face love's defeat.
I scroll through your pictures and press delete.
We can't deny our imperfections
Any more than we deny the connection.
I took your cards, your letters,
and discarded them on the streets.
Now I fight the urge to call.
I'm disturbed by this fall.
I cheated. I lied. I disconnected. Disrespected.
Neglected my responsibility
to never leave you feeling unprotected.
I missed you. Adored you. Dismissed you. Ignored you.
But learned quick and early on that even I
could afford to...fail.
It's always fun in the beginning.
Until you lay tired and broken...
Searching for a will to remain open.
I had to take a chance, knowing through all this I
could lose you.
I overstand now
You'll always see this the way you choose to.
Opposites attract and our differences are what made us.
I found myself in you in the same places
you'd find yourself in me.
But I knew you'd be discovered

the minute I walked away.
You're a precious jewel
I know now I can no longer keep a secret.
I won't apologize for being a dreamer
Or always thinking the grass is greener.
Though, I am sorry I failed to make you
See why I appreciate you.
All I ever did in the end
Was make you cry in the midst of our fights.
I sat and watched you drift away,
Out of my reach like satellites.
I miss my friend. My lover.
My soulmate. My companion.
I will never regret the sense of pride
You instilled in me at the Grand Canyon.
We made a mess of our home
Not suited for mops and brooms.
We only hurt each other, these day
And continue to scratch at open wounds.
So, tell me what is the point in digging up a
casket from its tomb?
I suppose believing in love is just as silly
As it is human will to chase the moon.
All I can do is observe these words
like an impartial spectator.
You loved me unconditionally...
With no apologies and blissfully.
First hand we are learning the difference
Between feeling normal and being cordial.
Second hand we are being forced to mold
A future that is untold.
The thought of someone else touching you,
making you smile
Eats away at my core.

But we are healing sores and closing doors
And I don't want to hurt you anymore.
I just hope you'll remember me the most
Through our love and simple giving.
I cope by finding peace
In our values and simple living.
You say I've invaded your blood, your soul...
Your essence.
But the Universe is also forcing us not to ignore
What is present.
Every single time you think of me, I feel it...
No matter where I am.
But I just can't face you,
You hurt too badly in more ways than one.
This would either make or break us.
Take us to places we've never been.
My attempt at solitude only showed me
You'll always live beneath my skin.
All I have is my love, my flaws, and my guitar.
No degree. No money. No promises. No car.
I still dream... even through pain...
Remembering nights you'd scream my name.
With that said I still want to take you to Japan
And scribe our names into the sand.
Conversation and mental elation
That cannot be found elsewhere.
A woman whom once served as competition
To even the best healthcare.
Though new people are in our systems,
I know we still think of each other
when we are with them...
For I see now nothing that is mine
will ever be lost from me.
Even in the midst of all confusion,

We are prone to illusions of love...
Even when we think we are done.
Even when we think we've had enough.
Like two binary stars in orbit,
That'll never touch unless they must.
No room for "shoulda woulda couldas"
The Universe has done this for us.
Everyone around us believed in this,
despite all that happened.
So, I turn my back unable to face
the repercussions of my actions.
Even if I can't have you to myself
I'll learn to love without ego.
Even on the days I'm near a phone...
For some things are better off left unknown.
Enough hurtful things have been said.
All that we could do has been done.
But this is the poem you've always wanted
For, now I know you're the one.
We will be together again someday
even if not in this form.
Drowning in the love we've always wanted...
An undying love that will again be confronted.

The Faithful Unfaithful

My ex-fiancé once told me cheating
isn't the end all be all.
That there are worse things you can do
to someone you love.
That's funny...
Cause, the minute I showed interest in someone else
It somehow implied to her she wasn't enough.
From the moment I noticed you,
my intentions were to grow with you
But I told you from day one I was in a bad place.
And, you accepted it.
You accepted my evolution
despite the pain of my past being all over my face.
I've made mistakes. I've cheated and been defeated.
Been in the position of having a cake
and I'd always eat it.
It never ended well cause monogamy was their norm
And, it was something in which I found
I couldn't conform.
For a long time I was convinced
something was wrong with me.
That cheating simply meant I couldn't handle
commitment.
But I'm a lover and although I love "different",
never in my life have I been on some pimp shit.
I love too hard, so I don't do one-night stands.
Nor do I sleep with anyone just because I can.
At the same rate, I was always down on myself
because I could hardly meet
my woman's faithful demands.
I love you. I love you enough to be honest.
Most of the time I'm celibate

and don't want to be bothered.
But, the fact of the matter is
if you could credit me with infidelity
I would have a number of degrees indebted to me.
I'm learning there is no right or wrong way
to be with someone.
I'm not a fan of polyamory but I respect it.
It forces you to face yourself,
the value of connections and
I know you're here to teach me that lesson.
Do we have multiple soul mates? I, mine and you, yours?
Can we have multiple lovers
as long as we return home to each other?
I try to read between the lines
but it appears I am illiterate
Because, to you I've been nothing but inconsiderate.
I mean...
What's the point of having a cake
if you can't eat it, though?
Does the saying imply I already have a piece of pie?
I'm not needy or greedy, I just walk in my highest truth
and I'm in a place now where I don't feel I need to lie.
But polyamory is isolated like apartheid.
People believe it means you have issues, a dark side...
But there are those who believe monogamy
isn't our nature
And, if it's subjective then which one is correct?
It doesn't matter to me. You're all that matters to me.
And, this confession is my first lesson,
whatever our matters may be.
I do value monogamy. I've successfully done it.
But, no matter the type of love you have
there's something to learn from it.

Now I get my ex. It wasn't the cheating; it was the lying.
It was my dismissal of her feelings
despite the fact she was trying.
She tried to forgive me,
but just placed the ring back in my hand...
Simply because I couldn't explain something then
that I now understand.
That all you need for me to do
is be fair and present with you...
And, not give in to my tendency to push away.
I don't know if I'm the relationship type
but as I get closer to truth,
I realize other women just help me feel closer you.
Monogamy or polyamory.
In which would you need to be complacent?
If you don't have a strong foundation,
it's a lose-lose situation.
No matter the circumstances, we're all taking chances.
Different people just love differently and that's okay.
Instead of choosing one
I would truthfully rather be alone
but I'm not going anywhere...
Even if you cheat, too.
I repeat: I am not going anywhere.
I just need you to trust me like you need me to trust you.

Surrender

I take responsibility. I acknowledge.
But you want me to keep doing it.
Apologies tend to expire
and you force me to keep renewing them.
Back me into a corner. Push my limits 'til I break
and retaliate.
Then you become the victim,
using my actions to validate.
Do you ignore what you do and say?
Do you take time to evaluate?
I have to learn to calibrate.
Being you are quite tough to navigate.
I know I've made mistakes. I used to take and allocate.
But you see me trying to be better
and surround me by rattlesnakes.
You'd rather yell and call me names.
Show disregard for my belongings.
We cautiously maneuver through us,
feeling justified in our wronging's.
Yet, I'm a coward for wanting to leave.
I'm supposed to take you ripping me to shreds.
All I do is lie and deceive.
Deserving treatment as the monster in your head.
You wonder why I'm invisible in bed.
And, you're convinced you've given your all.
I'm neither abuser nor victim here.
As it took us both to build this wall.
I don't know much about Love or commitment
and its definitely shown in us.
I just know communication is big.
So, is security. So, is trust.
Romance is an ongoing process

and we must learn together and forgive.
At this point we've done the worst.
What else to do but learn and live?
I'm human. I'm remorseful
but to you I've never been resourceful.
I've been controlling and unfair,
but my Love is no Morse code.
I'm left with bruises on my face,
you with bruises on your heart.
We both drown in resentment,
in seas overlooked by sharks.
We agree that space and counseling is needed
and a good start.
Yet, I'm selfish for focusing on my life. My art.
How can I contribute to us
if I am not contributing to myself?
At some point I have to resort
to looking out for my own health.
Despite your attacks and discrediting,
I have loved you the best way I can.
We both brought pain into this
but if it's not your way it'll never stand.
Nothing I do or say is good enough.
Armed with women and info of my past.
We're best friends but enemies.
Back and forth between tears and laughs.
All you've done is null and void
once I act in self-defense.
I'm then responsible for my own actions
but yours are up to me to prevent.
I've never had to be here...
Quarreling and hurting with such intent.
You know me best, you're convinced.

I feel trapped. Condensed.
There is no more room for healing.
There is no more room for respect.
These fighter jets are aimed to wreck
but only one of us can eject.
We sit in silence with this virus.
Taking wheels from cars without mileage.
Too much damage has been done.
I am traumatized by this violence.
Never did such things 'til I met you.
But I won't blame you for what's now behind us.
My past is your knife in war
and my shields just blind us.
We've shared so many great things
and had much purpose in each other's lives.
You've grown a lot though still growing
and I've been worthless to your life.
That's what you claim so maybe it's time we move on.
Divide and conquer.
I see in you all the good I've given
so I accept that I'm the monster.
I know now you were my biggest lesson yet.
And, I thank the universe for this release.
For, now I can truly have happiness.
Face myself and make peace.
I would have liked you to reap the benefits
of who I'm evolving to be.
To you, my poetry is an illusion
But these words are karma setting me free.

Breaking patterns and relearning me...
I surrender.

<u>Sun Salutations</u>

It's the perfect day for new beginnings.
I like making you laugh more than making you smile.
If I had known you wouldn't be here this morning
I'd have prevented last night from getting hostile.
And, instead held you in all your spirit.
Arms 'round the unhealed parts of your being.
Until all this Love you've denied yourself
Left you forgiving. Left you agreeing.
I'd love you until it was freeing.
Until it was secure and guaranteeing.
I'd love you until it had meaning.
Until you were led to say you weren't leaving.
Today your scent is still in my sheets.
You left your butterfly earring on my shelf.
I burn sage to clear the tears.
I can still feel how yesterday felt.
If I had known I'd love you this much
I'd have tried more to put it into practice.
If had known we'd have it this rough
I'd have changed the ways we've adapted.
Cause, yelling and screaming just isn't my thing
And, it will never be as of today.
If I had known I'd end up doing it here
I'd have found much better eggs to lay.
I miss you today. I'll miss you tomorrow.

I'll miss you even when all of this is fixed.
If I had known we weren't leaving together
I would not have wasted all of those trips...
I'd instead have tasted all of your lips
And, gave face to all in your hips.
I'd have tied you up in my compassion
Bounding you with Love's chains and whips.
If I had known you carry so much hurt
I'd have taken more time to learn your language.
I'd have been gentler toward the both of us.
Releasing us from pain and anguish.
If I had known I'd become your enemy
That you'd hold grudges and keep me at bay.
I'd have painted forgiveness on your tragedy
And, wished you well along your way.
We never know just why we pray
Just as one never knows why they stay.
If I had known we'd be fools in Love
I'd have found healing words to convey.
I'll miss you today. I'll miss you tomorrow.
I'll miss you well after no more of this.
If I had known I'd love you this much.
I'd have known when to call it quits.
This Love Jones had us bending.
Contending. Defending. Then ending.
And, on this morning of new beginnings
I must make sure to keep ascending.

Eclipse (Reflections on Love)

The greatest love I ever had was in writing about it...
It seems there is always a weight to lift
after had relationships.
Moments I prefer to occur just never seem to occur
and it only results in my writing words to be heard.
But, I'm not in the business of changing perceptions...
And, I'm tired of battling with heart shaped weapons.
So never mind what people of my past think of me...
I've grown on my own just through acceptance.
Yet these lessons call for reflections and I must say,
we are all to blame.
Love doesn't need you to believe in it
cause if you're breathing it's one in the same.
I've given hours and gotten back minutes.
Held on to nothing when the other was finished.
And, I've had to call myself out on the fact
that I love too hard yet am a cynic.
For heartache there are no clinics.
No such thing as hospitals or doctor visits.
You... are left to deal with a sickness
that only you yourself can diminish.
And, there are times I should have done that
but I didn't...
We just rebound and transfer feelings.
Too afraid to be alone and face Self,
unaware that is the best healing.
We... blame love and say it sucks.
We... base love on finding luck.
We close doors and instead of opening others,

we just prefer to keep them shut.
But, maybe some of us are happier alone
and miserable when involved.
It doesn't mean something is wrong with us,
or that we have problems yet to be solved.
We assume that people in solitude
-- those that that find comfort in independence --
Either, fear Love, have been hurt,
or see it as a prison sentence.
We give some people a mile
and they're only grateful for inches.
So, maybe they're tired of playing games
and prefer to sideline it on the benches.
Either way, Love is just one of those things
we all have to experience...
Whether it's family, friends,
romance or learning to love ourselves.
We are quick to blame Love,
for it is something we claim to fully understand.
But human beings are always changing
and flaws are a fallacy of man.
People get images of you in their head
and confine you to their obligations.
Get mad, hurt, and dismiss you
when you don't meet their expectations.
There are those who don't love themselves
and need others to do it for them.
Many have killed themselves.
Got all up in arms when folks ignore them.
Love brings out the best and worst in me

and although that has hurt to see...
I've learned Life and Love does go on
well beyond burns to the third degree.
With... harassment due to attachment
We have bitter days and bitter ways.
But through it all I am grateful
Being now, more thankful than hateful.
So, when breaking up leads to making up
or singing "Good Morning Heartache"
when you're waking up...
I keep in mind the Universe is always in balance.
All the women in my past served a purpose
that was important to me at that time.
Can't control my fate on soul mates,
So, I have learned to leave them behind.
If tomorrow comes and Love is no longer shared,
care for you. Be prepared.
Love just is and doesn't always seem fair.

But it *is* always there.

Doing Me

I have the ability to disconnect.
I can go years without sex.
And, the most liberating thing I've learned about myself
is that I've never really loved anyone.
I use these honest words to empower me,
Coming of actions that once were cowardly.
Knowing there is much I can accomplish without the
help of an accomplice.
I've done things I can't take back
And, I have come to face that.
But it doesn't mean I'll never love again or that I don't
deserve to be loved.
I let this feeling pass through me
As I work toward a new me.
For, loving myself better means I can love others, truly.

So, do you.
I'll do me.

<u>Karma</u>

I've witnessed women go from Buddha to Medusa.
And, I think "You'd really marry me
in all this vulgarity?!"
It's like... mentally I was sure we were meant to be.
Then she turns out to be the worst of my enemies.
Surrounded by darkness
of our own destructive entities;
Through many lifetimes, decades, and centuries.
Trying to break this karma. Intentionally...
But, I guess our egos still aren't small enough.
Selfish. Unfair... We were all of the above.
When that Jones comes down
one can't resist falling in love.
Passing judgment and being critical...
Chipping away at each other's peace.
Left with hearts battered and beat
when she's all that mattered to me.
The only logical obstacle I can think of
Is perhaps my own insight.
I'll fly sky high on Love then lose my wings in flight.
Never quite finding the right words
to speak from my windpipe...
So, I give into whatever my pen writes.
When it comes to interconnectedness,
We dance in ecstasy.
Especially, with our destiny
'Til we come to accept that s--t.
So, maybe we'll finally learn and do better next lifetime.
If not, that's okay...
I write my best poetry when in pain.

OG Kush

I found myself in reflection
While rolling up some Kush, today.
I began to think about past lovers.
Mostly the ones I've pushed away.
I love hard. I love openly.
And, I fully respect relationships.
Although I stay rooted in Love
I tend to wreck relationships.
I break hearts. They break mine.
And, we walk away with much resentment.
For, me to later fathom my actions
And, come to know my own contentment.
So, perhaps that is just Love...
Cycles of mistakes and attaining wisdom.
I light this Kush in non-judgment
Just vibing along to Love's rhythm.

Horns of Saturn

They say practice makes perfect
but you can't interpret a well-known song
unless you first hear it yourself.
Musicians aren't born overnight, so...
We learn of Utopian notes from instrumentals.
Playing instruments we can't afford.
Taking lessons and we end up settling for rentals.
I am just causing myself more pain
by pretending I don't know some names.
Lately I've been acting strange,
truth is I've had a hard time welcoming change.
I've had my heart broken,
drowning in these radio waves
Wondering how we went from worshipping suns
to fighting over funds.
I had a chance with her and I danced with her.
I write my wrongs to right my wrongs.
Feeling that vibration as I write these songs.
Believing with me is where she still just might belong.
Hearing that bass and that treble, now.
Knowing it wasn't in me to settle down
Yet, I still put a ring on her finger.
Made her heart sing better than singers.
She said she never had a woman like me.
I said I never had a woman 'til you.
Now, it's unlikely that I might be the one for you.
They say music is the last form of transcendence.
So, I welcome these horns,
realizing maybe it is crazy to believe in unicorns.
Brother Jupiter. Father Sun. Lover Mars.
Take me to Venus. Take me beyond these scars.
I need natural sparks like the same ones you gave Tesla.
Saturn's stress, the... music is speaking to me.
I'm getting sick and tired of being sick and tired.
Dating victims and liars.
These mannequins and their shenanigans.
I'm on a quest to be taken much higher

and her levels have too many limits.
And, her shovel had nothing in it.
But she kept digging and digging. And, digging...
Coming up empty handed.
I've been hurt and I've been the one to hurt.
Neither position is quite in demand.
It's unfortunate that her shape was proportionate
to the rings that surround her spinning body.
Keeping me cycles of self-doubt and discomfort.
I let it move through my body like techno
And, out of my system like strep throat.
Every time I hear these horns I know I have to let go.
You can't please everyone,
just like you can't see every Sun so...
I choose to shine regardless and evolve.

If you've hurt anyone, forgive yourself.
Even if they don't forgive you.
You can't live them. You have to live you.
And there is absolutely nothing
you cannot live through so...
Forgive them even if they are unapologetic.
Saturn will have its way with them so let it.

Saturn is the force of fate
that calls for you to experience your karma.
Listening to the tunes
Closing Pandora's box on his satellite moons.
The Universe is pure math
and 1+1 isn't always absolute.
Measures begin and end with you
and in numbers, there is truth.

I never thought I'd kiss a face again.
Never thought I'd share a space again.
Never thought that I would love again...
But, I did.

<u>Honor</u>

When there is nothing one can do
But, let things be.
I send Love to those I've hurt
And, that also means me.
My father always told me
There's no price on peace of mind.
I am martyr for all the bread
I've sliced to leave behind.
I've broken bread for my past.
Paid the price for those before me.
I now have nothing left.
To feed pain in all its glory.
So, I write to give way.
I create for forgiveness.
The grass is green on both sides
Never mind the bridges.
I've crossed them blind in darkness.
Walked them among the heartless.
I know time will speak essence
To all lessons, regardless.
I forgive those who danced with me
And, left me to my tunes.
I forgive me for cosmic voyages.
Leaving Lovers on the Moon.
Facing demons toward higher selves.
We are all growing and learning.
Letting go like we're supposed to
While the world continues turning.
To those I've shared bliss and pain
While journeying my Earthly tours
Just know I only left to honor my path
And, yours.

Mountaineer

I am

Chipping away at mountains.

Moving them is too much on my heart.

I need frequent breaks doing this cardio.

And, you'd usually be right here beside me.

Now it's just me and these boulders.

With the weight of my failures on my shoulders.

And, I'm only getting older

Yet, still I love like a Mountaineer.

Climbing and ascending…

Many prefer to reach the peak alone.

So, I push for the summit all on my own.

What doesn't kill you makes you strong.

I hike trails that make me sweat it out.

Allow me to forgive others and myself.

Now, the same mountain that caught my fall for you

Is providing lessons in Self-Love.

"Seek the path that demands your whole being" –Rumi

Haikus

The Art of Syllables

I laugh behind drums.

I laugh behind drums.
Finding fun in the rhythm
And, rhythm in fun.

Hip Hop is not dead.
But, given its influence
The ego should be.

Daddy doesn't care.
I just imagine he's there
When I recite poems.

I love hard like brick.
Not sure I know how to love.
My buildings collapse.

The scent of ocean.
Sunrise across Tybee shores.
Makes me miss Georgia.

Graffiti on trains.
Moving along like her hips.
Our life in the Bronx.

I miss her father.
That man loved me like his own.
Someday I will be.

What you see in me.
Good or bad, you now see you.
We are reflections.

Women of my past
Have just shown me the way.
Helpers on my path.

When you transmit "God"
Avoid interference from
Religion's static.

Never knew my hair
Could grow to be long & strong
When it's natural.

Shedding tears and things.
I give up all attachments
Just to gain myself.

Closet door creaks shut
After the baggage escaped.
Skeletons exposed.

At just 2 years' old
I would say to my mother
"I feel like a boy"

Back when I was 3
I first kissed another girl.
I knew then. I knew.

Bold and courageous.
I take risks and learn lessons
In humility.

Logic is not all.
Some things lie outside our grasp.
Man will learn someday.

Visit her often.
She's 22 years of me.
My love. Chicago.

Yesterday has died.
Tomorrow has yet to birth.
Embrace the moment.

Mountains speak to me
Along the way of a climb.
Words translate high up.

Want to know someone?
Why read a biography?
Actions tell you all.

Love astronomy.
Views divine through telescopes.
The study of "God".

With skeletal frame.
Among broken bones and shame.
I hide in closets.

I worry my mom
Loses sleep over her kids.
And, I'm the baby.

I love you like class.
But there is so much to learn.
Teachers are students.

When I close my eyes
My 3rd eye then takes the wheel.
We park and sit still.

Clocks tick hourly.
Through cowardly time travel.
Lost my direction.

Armed love with duct tape.
Late at night, I sit and watch.
Then kidnap your heart.

School has showed me that
I was better off debt free.
College is a scam.

Society says
Without things you are nothing.
Buddha must be wrong.

All of my exes
Have since grown into greatness
Of course, due to me.

I am not changing.
Just becoming more of me.
Evolving throughout.

Life is like aircraft.
The first time I flew solo
I then understood.

Bending glass and time.
Too heavy on my frail heart.
She was a cynic.

I love solitude.
Not as much as I love her.
So, we compromise.

Happiness alone
Beats being in love's presence
When you won't face fears.

She has shown me that
Being "happier alone"
Is just an excuse.

My dear Black Women
You have no competition.
You are beautiful.

Have you seen my heart?
I have been looking for it.
She took it and ran.

Mornings I lay here
Full of regret and sorrow.
Gotta let her go.

Carried by nature.
As the Earth turns to greet her
I wait for the Sun.

Clipped wings. Broken backs.
Killing 2 birds with no stones.
Glasshouse for lovers.

The philosopher
Who accepts he knows nothing
Inspires me most.

Distracted by thoughts.
Out of brain when in the mind.
Nevermind your mind.

I learn to accept
Through surrender & patience.
How to truly live.

I bang on drum sets.
Uniting mind and body.
My meditation.

I travel the world
To meet who I've known before
And, have forgotten.

If blood is thicker
Then it must've been sustained.
We're all family.

A divine presence.
This is what remains in you
After Ego Death.

I am everyone.
I am everywhere, always.
I am everything.

Live a thousand times.
We are immortal beings.
No one ever dies.

Ready for take-off.
Radio transmit tower.
Life is a runway.

Do a 180
360 degrees of love.
It comes full circle.

This is food for thought.
I must eat more carrots.
Can't see in the dark.

It is hard to love
In a world full of thunder.
You are the quiet.

When it rains it pours.
As long as we're holding hands
We'll weather the storm.

My dearest ego.
Let's go away together.
So I can kill you.

Life stuck on a bridge.
Instead of crossing over
I'd rather jump off.

Sets like two suns.
With 20/20 vision
They rise in her eyes.

Sensitive to feel.
Fingertips for us Lovers.
Touch the moon and sun.

Drown in your water.
Sunken ships that wear my name.
You taste like the Earth.

Meaning of Happy?
What does it mean to be free?
Who knows? It just means.

This love is quite rough.
Like friction to sandpapers
Rub 'til all smooth's out.

If it was not real
I would not be a writer.
Depression exists.

Waves of pain. Seasick.
I jump in and bottom out.
Life anchor detached.

Highway catharsis.
I drive with no direction.
Roundhill and downhill.

I'm trees standing tall.
Like northern Cali wildfires.
Deadwoods for Redwoods.

If tears are for queers
Then I will cry a thousand times.
No one knows my pain.

When your shields block light
You live in complete darkness
10 miles from the Sun.

Like pens to cloud 9
An unstable atmosphere
Creates thunderstorms.

If this is my gift
Writing in past tense, I can't
Enjoy the present.

Like a Buddhist Monk
In 3rd eye meditation:
Become connected.

Back against the wall.
With "God" in my corner
I don't fear boxes.

I am free because
Resumes' don't define me.
The Universe does.

Women of my past
Have since taught me 1 lesson:
I am not my past.

With dangerous eyes
She can give me just one look.
I turn to rubber.

When tables turn
It's cold turkey on both sides.
Good karma served fresh.

Such platters taste good
To those who wash dishes.
Food for thought. Eat up.

Pupils dilated.
The dark seas and the dark sees.
Tears stream before dreams.

Battle without war
Be the peaceful warrior.
Open heart. Clear mind.

Man-made dilemmas?
Seek refuge in the mountains.
Your essence is there.

Dead stars gave us life.
Camera flash. Shine. We go from
Dead stars to dead stars.

The very fact that
I'm willing to marry her
Speaks. Despite my past.

Eyes like brown sugar.
The loveliest things I've seen
Next to her lips.

Brown eyes like heaven.
Wings crouched in her business suit.
Angel in Disguise.

Freestyle marathons.
Love is only for swimmers.
Its waters run deep.

She's like the mountains.
Perfect carve and elevation.
Always ascending.

Love reflects on us
Like skies reflect on water.
We are reflections.

Do not fear the cold.
Lovers in high altitudes
Close in on the Sun.

She walks on water.
Not of the holy spirit
But, of her spirit.

"Why do you like me?"
You're a sunrise to the eye
And, truth to the lie.

Leave mistakes behind.
The present is a present
And, a gift, you are.

Whenever it's done
Let it be completely done.
Back and Forth? No Fun.

Nothing just happens.
It's universal balance.
Life is a challenge.

What you see, you get.
But, looks can be deceiving.
Some hide in plain sight.

Bright prism of skin.
A rare, precious pot of Gold.
She's from the rainbows.

Ancestral visions
Date me back to Egyptians.
Our brown skin in Gold.

We love all Black men.
We push on and fight for them.
Where is our support?

A mother is all.
As defined by her children.
Dictionary Love

Jumping off of cliffs
Is only scary when you
Don't know you have wings

I would like to think
That everything is better
With hip hop & weed

Nature nurtures life
I find peace in mountains and
Answers to questions

If I died today
It wouldn't be the first time
Young or old. That's life.

Death is upon me.
But this is more spiritual.
Rebirth in the mind.

This pain I feel now
Is learning from the past and
Healing the future.

Suicidal thoughts
Are racing all through my mind.
I win. Finish line.

This healing work we do
Are the 9 to 5s of "God".
Pain is illusion.

It's plain and simply.
You are safe and you are loved.
I want you. Let go.

Sex complicates things.
So does living. So does love.
Now is all we have.

If Love is a drug
Then I def need rehab
I'm high off this shit

Desert time travel
Nature's mysterious eye
I've gone through portals

She is the sunset.
Of views to a mountain's peak.
Heat rising to Love.

Eyes like therapy.
A body like medicine.
She's art. She's healing.

A voice like smooth jazz.
Her smile is therapeutic.
My wellness-practice.

Rhythm bass and drums.
Pulling strings on her mental.
She is/makes the music.

Can't always read her.
Still admire from a distance.
Her heart's library.

Can't always read her.
Still admire from a distance.
Her mind's library.

The rhythm and blues.
Open her like a new book.
Lessons in her Love.

Four legged felines
Always a good companion
In your darkest days.

Pit Pat on the floor
I had a cat named Drummer
With drum sticks for paws.

Relationship Fail
I end up missing our cat
More than I miss her.

I love to travel.
Hate flying over water.
So, it's bittersweet.

I'm from Chicago.
Where Blacks find joy in all pain.
Like sunshine to rain.

Moon. Stars. Water. Peace.
Smoking weed at the lakefront.
These Chicago nights.

No options. No hope.
Poverty is policy
In West Englewood.

Down the lineage.
Generational trauma
In the blood of us.

Our ancestors died
Hoping we would rise again.
We're their wildest dreams.

Nightmares of war
On the streets of Chicago
Dreams haunted by grief.

Soldiers versus goons
Battling our own demons.
Which side am I on?

A dangerous woman.
Crave her like I crave Life.
She's the death of me.

Though not of this Earth.
Damaged and full of this world.
A wounded Goddess.

Forces of Nature.
Earth. Fire. Wind. Water. Heart.
Captain of planets.

Energy can't die.
Can only be transferred. Changed.
So, Love endlessly.

Freedom
Poems

The Aviator

Clear your fear of heights and take this flight

Love Birds

Clear your fear of heights and take this flight

Along side me.

Your wings were once clipped...

And, love was lost among the sky.

At the mercy of your heart...

You spread your wings and shed the pain.

The view is better up here, anyway.

Flying by faith, rather than sight.

<u>I Am Her Pilot</u>

She was born to fly.
So indigenous, this woman.
And I...
Only I...
Can take such a phenomenon to the sky.

I am her pilot.
Shifting paradigms of our dynamic.
An addicted manic for the sky...
A manic for her panoramic.

Strong wings of an eagle.
The body of an Angel.
Smooth air flows over her surface...
We take off to climb out at a perfect angle.

She breathes out. I breathe her in.
Driven by a motor of love intuition.
Exhale. Inhale...
An engine that will never fail...

She is the aviator of my cognition.
I, the pilot of her thought.
I take flight within her mind.
Gain altitude within her soul.

I am her pilot.
Though on ground, she remains among clouds.

Gently, she speaks to me
No matter how loud...
The wind.
From turbulence she protects me...
It is her I fly within.

I am her pilot.
Run my hands among her genuine
Feminine structure.

Never will she let me crash.
Intense rush of adrenaline. I touch her...
Controls, as her wheels roll
Full throttle to my heart beat.
Destination: Love. As we rise above...
The rough surface of life's concrete.

I shall remain insatiable, until able to...
Clear her free of life's runway.
Given the chance we'll climb toward heaven...
Monday through Sunday.

I am her pilot.
We never land from such realistic
Simplistic flight.
Forever dualistic...
We'll fly away like birds
Into the mystic
Of the night.

Untitled

I was practicing landings today,

And, happened to witness a shooting star.

Its trail streaked across the blue sky,

Leaving its fragments within the atmosphere.

I closed my eyes...

Wind. Soft. Quiet. Calm.

...And it was perfect timing.

Aligning both the Moon and Sun in shining.

White clouds formed just over the horizon.

Felt the Universe inside me,

Surrounding my being.

Wondered if I would ever experience God

that way again.

Didn't want to land,

Risking such a chance.

I just wanted to fly away within that moment

Of forever.

Such an internal...

Eternal...

Sensation.

It reminded me of you.

Black Aviator

On the south side of Chicago
There appears to be one way.
Monday through Sunday
You must be weary of gunplay.
Where some lack in education
But dream to make it out someday.
Where you don't see Blacks in aviation
Yet I choose life on the runway.
Every time I'd board a plane
My kind was not in the captain seat.
And because of that I just figured
There were other things I'd have to be.
But when I looked into our history
I began to question those beliefs.
I read up on Bessie Coleman
And realized all is within reach.
I felt so weightless and free
The first time I ever flew solo.
It's like the sky was made for me.
And, everything moved in slow mo.
I'm paving roads for the no names
With payback in such incentives.
Spent my parent's money with no shame
Cause flight training is expensive.
But, no matter how hollow my means
I pursued and followed my dreams.
Finding light in darkness I come from
And sharing it with Chicago's teens.
Today I go full throttle
Rotate before the runway's finish.
With cloud 9 at my wingtips
I know now, the sky has no limit.
So on the south side of my city.
Where many feel they have no options.
Trailblazers emerge from struggle.
I'm here. A black woman in the cockpit.

The Goddess

I am in love with Mother Earth.

Black Woman

I am in love with Mother Earth.
From a smooth tongue she speaks.
Words hit me like bullets,
For she aims at me with wisdom's gun.
Whispering metaphors of seduction,
In the protection of my arms.
I kiss her neck...
The scent of enticement.
I touch her skin...
The softest silk.
Lay her on her stomach, she smiles...
As I run my tongue down her spine.
Watching her back muscles flex,
Using bodily movements as validation.
Turn her over...
And between her thighs,
Lies the sweetest taste of brown sugar.
Biting her bottom lip, clinching the sheets...
So cinematic.
I am an addict.
Then as I enter she sways those hips,
That have the ability to move oceans.
Causing tsunamis flowing beyond my shoreline.
Sweat drips,
From these bodies of water.
A radio is not needed...
We are already in harmony.
Her moans sing me jazzy melodies,
In tune to the rhythm of my thrusts.
She closes her eyes but views me,
Clearly.
Hands become her vision.
Creating our own wind, she sees my heart.
I tell her again and again that I love her.
Deep breaths,
I kiss her forehead.
Brown legs wrapped around my pelvic frame.
Wavelengths of love floating throughout the air.
I run my fingers in and out of her locs.
Seconds become minutes and minutes, hours...
I can listen to this music forever.
In unison, we slow dance into the night.
She is my African Queen.

Reach

She walks so gracefully.
Feet not touching the ground
as she glides toward me with elegance.
Defying gravity of the very things that hold her down.
Hips swaying to the rhythmic drum beats
of her ancestors.
She wraps her hair with the essence of Nefertiti.
Giving her love but never freely...
Narrow heartbeats of a pharaoh
Who is no longer in rule of her dynasty.
Lady of Grace. Queen of her Nile.
Where upstream rivers flow down her thighs...
Not knowing what it is like to truly smile...
Among these night streets that seem to keep her alive.
Though she has died a few times already,
For she is so broken,
rebirthing in slow motion on this quest to feel alive.
She doesn't live. She survives.

Egyptian Goddess.
She's dipped in the hottest fire one could ever burn.
Her spirit sings its own opera.
She's a fool to vodka and ruled by her sacral chakra.
Hips moving to the rhythm of painful melodies.
Where men have committed felonies...
And, simply walked away.
Taking with them love
she never received from father figures.
So, demons in her garden
plant family ties of rotten fruit.
A Nubian heartbreaker.
Sex is her alchemy as partaker in her walk of truth.

She sees things...

Animals and shapes that whisper
to her clues of her gifts
In the spirit of healing.
Pleasure and pain tattooed on her inner thighs.
She meditates for an inner high.
Rolling blunts to reach heights of kings and queens
From her collapsing pyramid schemes.

She knows when the mountains speak,
Like her voice in range
bouncing off the mountain's peaks.
Hips with rhythmic natural mystic
defying laws of physics...
When she wants them to.
She's been homeless yet so homeful,
lying in the bed of Mother Africa
Walking trails of free thought
for those who come after her
As a halo type aurora shines
just above her Earthly temple.
Loving her can be as easy as she lets it be.
She's beautifully captivating.
Heart chakra activating on the eyes of others.
There is no coincidence
to the infinite amount of lovers... she has.
If she ever crosses your path,
you will surrender to the tender touch of her energy.
She will give you no choice.
As she glides among Mother Earth... So gracefully.
Reaching... Searching...
For her (r)evolution.

Black Phoenix

Black womyn, I wanna tell you, you are beautiful.
You've been beaten down, broken and placed
at the bottom of the barrel.
Europeanized, staring down barrels of mental 45s...
Carrying demise of what is equivalent to 40 lives.
Mother of Kemet's first age.
Yet unwritten from history's first page.
The world's first Sage.
Now you assimilate to be acceptable.
Aiming to please those
that don't even respect your truth.
Still searching for Love
in those who gave up on protecting you...
Self-hate is reaching within...
Now you're bleaching your skin.
Because, society's microphone
has made way for lighter tones.
It's never easy when told you're told
you were never Nefertiti.
We are the many Queens
who have been murdered throughout time.
They've taken your history
and now they've come for your mind.
Murder the Queen. The darker your shades,
the less attractive you feel...
Supporting families as single mothers,
having been abandoned by your brothers.
You're too busy paying bills
to tend to wounds that won't heal.
Being led to perm your hair.
Your kinks and locs don't matter.
Yet, you are the missing puzzle piece
to the building blocks of matter.
Let your hair be your therapy.
Of a mind you dare to free.

Don't you dare hide behind
what you don't think they care to see.
And, never mind the Black men who don't love you.
They are the ones unwilling to admit
they don't love some part of themselves.
You are part of him and he is part of you.
Let him date whoever he wants
but he can't deny he started with you.
Don't believe them when they tell you you're unworthy.
Back bone like Nina Simone,
hair wraps and hips that are curvy.
You survived slavery, something I'm sure
they hate to see so...
Rise again and know it...You are beautiful.
Do it for the little Black girls
who are taught to doubt within.
Do it for the little Black boys
taught to doubt the outs of their skin.
The only way out is within
so birth love from your wounds.
You're a story untold so let the pages unfold.
Let it extend from your truffled and ripped out feathers.
Barefoot, we all walk this glass-covered path together.
From your divine feminine,
meditate on burning incense.
Reclaim your mind's innocence
toward self-love and remembrance.
As we return to emotion and wisdom
in the grasp of your soular system.
You shall unveil Mother Earth
from the hatred that covers her.
Be it with locs or bald fades
you look lovely in all shades,
So, rise from the ashes and tell them "I am beautiful".

<u>Sacred Drum</u>

She calls upon them.
Dances and hums them.
Honors and drums them...
Her ancestors.
Secrets of her history are the deepest of her mysteries.
This Mother Africa has been massacred.
Her voice. Her words have been silenced. Abbreviated.
For she is among many who are unappreciated.
Through nature, she regains her nomenclature
Moving her body through pain 'til it is alleviated.
You can feel the adrenaline through her divine feminine.
She returns us all to balance and innocence.
She dances for the breeze
She dances for the seas.
She dances to free...
All that is you and that is me.
As chakra colors of gold and green emit from her aura.
Her body writes the rhythms of its own Torah.
Blending harmonies and words with melodic crossfades
We chant "Ase'!" "Ase!". "Namaste!'"

Black womyn...
Gathering food in Earth's bowl...
Dancing all negativity from her soul.
Black womyn...
They can hear your healing cries.
And, from beneath the soil, they rise.

She's been over sexualized. "Extraterrestrialized".

For, she's been forced to carry the world
by weight of her back.
And as the sweat drips from her wet hips
She reminds us, all that is beautiful is Black.
With bones and stones you can hear the vibrations
As crystals join in rotation of her gyrations

Animals speak through visions of Shamanic eyes
Grasping Amethyst and Black Onyx, she rise.
They come around when sounds
from within her brown skin...
Are enough to leave us transcending Womyn's ending.
Swinging dreadlocks, marrying past,
present and future from wedlock.
As the djembe's energy brings out the inner me.
Creating... Goosebumps from her foot thumps
Windmills that send chills...
From wombs to tombs she brings forth life.
With this rhythmic, we dance unto kismet...
Between bass drums and her gift of foresight,

Black womyn.
Dance us back into existence
Release your pain through sweat as your body rinses.
Black womyn.
Dance until we get it
Reunite us to the spirit world through our senses.
Black womyn.
Free those defined by their linens.
Touch base with them, beyond the 9th inning.
Black womyn.
They can hear your healing cries,
And from beneath the soil, they rise.

(*For Qween Hollins*)

She is

She is 100 degrees Fahrenheit.
The sunshine in my paradise.
Blazing me to golden skin.
Pushing envelopes. Folding in.
She is Explorer in sailing seas.
Delivering my God's mail in threes.
She is a pyramid in Egypt.
Another lyricist to decrypt.
She is a canteen in the desert.
Bottles at shore of written letters.
She is nothing you thought she would be.
Yet she is everything to me.
She is all words and ideas.
Circling curves and high fears.
The wings you never know you have
'til realizing you've flown the path.
She is the light at the end of the tunnel.
A cosmos bound space shuttle.
That all around fresh morning feeling.
She is the moment you see your healing.
She is 1000 degrees Celsius
Among heart and mind's wealthiest
Grazing heat through golden skin.
Ancient sister. My golden kin.
Music connecting through interface...
Food for thought, my dinnerplate...
A continued test of my inner faith...
She is Love.

Black Energy

68% of the Universe.
She rises, overcoming gravity.
Accelerating expansion of the cosmos.
Unsure of how she operates
Unsure of what it all means
She outlines the emptiness of space.
Weak and strong forces of nature.
Carrying electromagnetic shields.
As more space emerges, so does Dark Energy.
She dominates.

Black Matter

27% of the Universe.
80% of its matter.
Light from her stars not yet arriving to Earth.
Dark and seen but unseen.
Un-noticed. Unacknowledged. Unobservable.
Yet, she holds the elements of the Universe together.
Groups of objects function together
through her explanations.
She rotates galaxies, filling them with her mass.
Where her stars orbit faster.
Holes in Black serve as gravity lenses and bend light.
Not normal matter. Not antimatter
She is Dark Matter.
The invisible hand of the Big Bang.

Parallels

I live in a world where everything is black and white.

Two Spirit

I live in a world where everything is black and white.
You're either this or that.
Nothing outside or in between.
Before I reached my teens
my brain was trained in these extremes.
A mental wall was even built
to separate kings from queens.
Boys wear blue. Girls wear pink.
Leave emotion to you. Leave it to men to think.
Women are weak cause women feel.
Men are strong cause men build.
I arrived on this planet
in my most natural androgynous form.
Yet, everyday I've been subjected
to man-made societal norms.
In a world where women
are to submit and let men be in control
I had to find my own place
since I don't fit in with gender roles.
Ever since I was small I knew I was different.
I was my mother's pride and joy
but I remember wishing I was a boy.
By the time I could dress myself
to when adolescence reached its peak
I began to express myself but was only seen as a freak.
It has been some long hard years
on this journey to be me,
I struggled with my identity 'til I found a home in LGBT.
Getting harassed and being stared at
just seems to be a part of who I am.
But androgyny has existed
throughout the history of man.
Before Europeans came with their religion

and their disease...
The Natives looked to beings like me
to meet the community's spiritual needs.
With psychic abilities, we were healers, metaphysicians
And, medicine men.
These androgynous souls referred to as "two spirits"
were evident then.
We weren't ostracized but monopolized
as village leaders in our existence.
We were social workers and adoptive parents,
and weren't seen as any different.
We were marriage counselors and communicators
beyond the lines of physical dimensions.
There was no "LGBT".
There was no separate community to mention.
So, what happened?
How did we go from being accepted to being neglected?
How did we come to be "sodomites"
from which we were praised and much respected?
We were glorified as seeing the world
through the eyes of both sexes.
Then, Europeans came along
with their standards and objections.
Females are submissive. Males are dominant.
Gender roles and standards are prominent.
Men give. Women receive.
Society just moves along with ease.
We've been shut out by man-made dogma
and forced to exist in gender confines.
Yet, there are still a billion "me's"
society now chooses to leave behind.
We're so caught up in distinctions,
the blacks and whites of stereotypes
We've forgotten that beyond gender, beyond titles...
We're all just light.

We're so much more than our physical bodies.
It doesn't always matter what you see.
For, even Buddha was a little feminine
and Jesus was as pretty as me.
I think it's interesting how those who hate me most
tend to have Bibles in hand.
Yet, their God speaks to me in a frequency
that supersedes what's written by Man.
I am strong and I wear pink.
I'm emotional but I also think.
I'm the yin and yang of those who have lied
just in order to survive.
The world will not stop spinning
just because beings like me exist.
It is a gift of the most high
to be one who relates to both sides.
Why should I be subjected to
and accused of morale famine?
When in the days of indigenous man,
they took us and made us Shamans.
I am nature and nurture.
My queerness has taught us to be fearless.
So, I won't deny my two spirit
for the uncomfortable who fear it.
I define my duality. I don't let others do it for me.
We come from different walks of life
and there is no specific walk that is right.
So, the next time you want to close a door.
The next time you want to put me in a box.
Keep in mind I specialize in keys.
Keep in mind I specialize in locks.
I am the gray area...
And, though I feel there are no boxes for me to check...
Don't be mistaken. I still look damn good in a dress.

<u>Testrogen</u>

When I go to the beach
I am not allowed to be topless.
When I go into the men's restroom
I am not allowed to be cockless.
Don't want to be a runway model
Nor, do I wish to play basketball.
Despite what you think
I don't wear a mask at all.
I'm a gender bender.
Somewhere inside me is a man.
I wear my androgyny well.
Even on my hands.
No gender identity issues
With DMT and mescaline.
I am simply 50% testosterone
And, 50% estrogen.

<u>Enough</u>

What is normal?
What does the average person look like?
Try to answer these questions without being influenced
by what
televisions and magazines have led you to believe.
Can you still answer, then?
All my life I've had to deal with something.
I am too skinny.
Too tall.
My feet are too big.
I only wear locs cause I think I'm "deep".
I only shaved my head cause I think I'm a man.
Too dark.
Too   light.
Too Black.
Too White.
Not Black enough.
Not White enough.
Queer = pedophile
= rapist, murderer, necrophiliac, and dog fucker, as well.
Too queer.
Not queer enough.
Not lesbian enough.
Too masculine.
Too feminine.
Not straight enough.
Asexual.
Still going to hell.
Queers can't make children

So, I'm worthless.
Not feminine enough.
Not masculine enough.
Too much of a poet.
Not enough of a slam poet.
Too smart for college.
Not educated enough.
Resume doesn't have enough credentials.
Not enough money in my bank account.
Basically, I'm too much.
Or not enough.
If I were to change everything about me
for the happiness of someone else,
I would cease to exist.
So, why not be me?
Everyone's an expert on my weight,
shoe size, sexuality, poetry,
life goals, and etc.
Everyone knows what I should be, if not what I am.
I may not be enough for you.
I may be too much for you.
But, I'm enough for me.

My Identity

To the men it concerns,

I am not writing this to confront you.
More so to say you're beautiful, but I don't want you.
I'm not trying to take your place.
Not even trying to front you.
Trust me when I say I do nothing I don't want to.
You think you have people like me all figured out...
I've been hurt in the past or I've been abused.
If not that, it must then be that I'm confused.
Cause, I don't like being a woman
or I must have daddy issues.
That's right...
I reject my femininity
cause I'm afraid to let a man get into me.
If I don't want your penis something is wrong with me
cause every woman craves masculinity.
But, there is a difference between
"masculinity" and "man".
A woman can be masculine.
A man can be feminine.
Gender expression is different from sex
In the same way sex differs from how you dress.
Having a vagina does not obligate that I clean, cook,
and walk around barefoot and pregnant for you.
If I walk into a room and you're threatened
by my presence
That says less of me and more about you.
I don't want to be a man.

I've learned I have to break this down
to the visually dyslexic.
Cause, if you think all it takes to be a man is clothing,
then you aren't giving yourself much credit.
I don't awake every morning
and dress for your comfort.
That's not something I'm obliged to do.
Some of you think I still belong in the kitchen
But, my existence does not belong to you.
Yes... It is possible for a woman to not want or need you.
And, no...
Lack of a man in her life
does not mean she has yet to meet you.
Don't let this defeat you...
There are plenty of women out there
who crave your stimulation.
That's just not me.
The only time I dated men was
when it was out of obligation.
Before you denounce me and drag my name
through the mud,
Have a conversation with me, then judge.
I'm not afraid of you. I don't hate you...
It's just not my fault my dominance intimidates you.
My identity does not belong to you.
I'm sick of getting harassed for being in my truth.
This poem is for the men that need to hear these words.
For, bullshit out of season bears no fruit.
Everyone is an expert on my sexuality
And, they babble on about all they think they know.
Thanks for reminding me I can't impregnate a woman

But, my response to you is "So?!?"
I'm sorry if my voice is too deep for you.
I've not been raped, wronged, or victim of a crime.
If you've tackled ex-homosexuals, that's fine...
Keep in mind, that's her journey. Not mine.
It is not my duty to wear skirts or give birth...
Androgyny has existed for thousands of years.
But, when it comes to history some of you don't bother,
and it just so happens I love my father.
I made a choice to be me. Not a choice to be queer...
You need lessons in gender expression.
It is not my intention to be socially abused and told that
I am confused.
Whatever issues you have, just let me be.
Let me take this up with my creator.
You're so busy trying to figure out what sex I am you
overlook that you
shouldn't give a damn.
I'm not fucking my cousins. I haven't killed anyone...
Being disrespectful is wrong to do.
I know exactly who I am. I don't need your help.
Cause, my identity does not belong to you.

I got love for y'all. Where's the love for me?

I Am A Stud

I used to get funny stares in locker rooms.
My classmates would turn away from me
as they would change clothes.
They were uncomfortable for it was known
I was that masculine woman.
The type of woman that wasn't welcome in their homes.
The type of woman that never wore panties or thongs.
The type of teenager who used to sag her pants
to her knees
So she could feel that cool breeze
Flow in and out of her boxers.
Hanes and Fruit of the Loom written
just under my navel.
Yes, I am that woman.
A wild child, having grew up in a house
full of feminine women.
A tomboy at heart yet an innocent little girl at mind.
Not knowing my act and repetitions
would become a definition.
This was new to me, as I grew to be...
A Stud.

Scribed into my blood at conception
I was never too soft not to roll around in dirt.
Never too hard not to cry when I was hurt.
I grew to be that woman.
No manicures or pedicures.
I became a deviation from the norm.
Getting complaints from women

Who claimed that I taint their image.
Looks of pity from guys,
Who think we disguise what it means
to be a man in their eyes.
We are despised,
Told we are far from the real thing.
Since there exists no woman who can take their place
And, there exists no woman who cannot like Men
They say we lie to get by and think
we compete with and imitate them.
Female friends who didn't want
to be seen with me in public,
Afraid of the rumors and lies
That would begin if seen in my presence.
Yet behind closed doors,
they became my lesbian whores.
Hiding me from their friends and parents.
They were too embarrassed to cherish...
My demeanor.
As long as it was kept a secret,
they'd reveal themselves to me.
I'm here...
And I am a Stud.

And, I wear the scars of every stud
that has come before me.
Enduring beatings that left them with broken ribs
and empty baby cribs.
I wear the scars of every stud that has come before me.
That stud that was told she could not raise a child
with a woman,

because she was not the man of the house.
Those studs that had to lie and use gay men as alibis,
standing arm and arm on wedding cakes.
Those studs that were told
they would never see the day
a woman legally weds another.
Studs that have been ostracized by co-workers
and disowned by their mothers.
I wear their scars.
"Ag". "Dom". "Stud". "Butch".
Whatever she called herself
as she stood upon a broken foot.
Shattered bones caused by those who do not
understand and said
"Look! I'm Just being me!"
Never allowing her pride to be took
Or her balance on this Earth to be shook.
I wear the scars of every stud
that through blood sweat and tears...
Worked hard for the chance for me to be... ME.
Studs that have been raped by men
who were trying to prove a point.
Studs that have been cursed
by the military and every church,
Then were forced to question their worth.
Studs that have to endure the rude
who see them as gender confused.
Studs that get hated on and disrespected
by some ignorant ass dudes.

We are pilots. We are lawyers.

We are doctors. We are cooks.
We are scientists. Musicians. Soldiers. We are books.
We've been through it all
and through it all we've learned to do it all.
I wear the scars of studs who date other studs
and have to be told by their own kind
that it doesn't make sense.
The studs that aren't too caught up in the label
to allow their woman to go down on them.
The studs who wore tuxedos to prom
and full suits to work.
The androgynous souls that Native "Americans"
see as Kindred spirits.
Studs that prove genetics are synthetic.
I am a Stud.
I have walked through many hallways
With braids, locs, and bald fades... Proud.
Though I've heard whispers from within the crowd.
With our low-pitched voices.
Tones deeper than our sisters'.
Everywhere we go we're mistakenly referred to
as "sir" or "mister".
Walking into public bathrooms
with our timberland boots.
Causing discomfort to those who suppose that we are
confused about the sign on the outside of the door.
Unable to fathom our identity so we are the enemy
when we step into their vicinity.
Causing straight women to become bi-curious,

for we touch with a softness.
Softer than a man's hands.
They can't resist the way we strap up
and perform better than any man can.
Studs who want their chest to stay flat.
Sporting snapbacks and wave caps.
Wearing ties and Stacy Adams to work.
Air force ones and fitted caps on weekends.
Us studs... We go through pain, tease, and torment.
Forced to be dormant, but dormant-more or less
it is for the best.
Cause I've tackled teen pressure
and took extreme measures,
To just be... who I... am.

Our bond is dying and it is time to revive it.
We must flip the bandwagon over
and school the kids who ride it.
Cause our existence is universal.
I don't go to any rehearsals for this shit.
This is isn't an outfit I put on for the act.
You can't wear this shit for a day
then hang it right back on your rack.
This isn't a pair of shoes that can fit anyone
who wants to wear them.
Cause I am a Stud.
You may not hear me on your mp3 or see me on MTV,
But I'm here, though people choose
to ignore our many talents.
With a stud state of mind in this day and time,
I refuse to wait in line to be heard.

It is our day to shine and it begins with these words.
Through the hesitance and negligence.
Having been viewed as some sort of freak show.
It's ok, cause WE KNOW.
And proudly I wear the scars,
PROUDLY.
We are infinite beings, existing by innocent means.
We are the ones who can implement
both queens and kings.
And if there is mystery in that
then you don't know the history of that.

I AM A STUD.

<u>Always (To the Black Man it Applies To)</u>

There is no "Gay Agenda"
There are just gay people
In every race, culture and ethnicity.
It has been this way since the beginning of time
And, will continue through 'til the end of time.
You want to claim Egypt
But, not the homosexuality that was taking place there.
This is not a trend.
This is not yet another thing to blame on the White man.
Homosexuality is not an attack on the Black man.
Before you come at Queers
about how they're hurting the community
Converse with us.
Ask questions with an open mind and heart.
Try listening.
While you're at it
Worry about the children you abandon
(That we often adopt and raise)
Worry about the Black women you leave hanging
And, the White women you worship and praise
While still policing us and telling us what to do.
What to wear.
How to act.
Dictating and complaining
about households you are not in.
Making every excuse not to be fathers to your children.
Or other's children
While you claim to be about unity and community.
Take responsibility for your own contributions

To the demise of your people.
These women don't fuck themselves
And, you don't give birth.
Both sides are responsible for single motherhood.
Plenty of these women raise straight men.
Plenty straight men raise gay sons.
There is plenty blame to go around.
Black gay men are not to blame for every damn thing.
We are not rubbing it in your face.
Not forcing it on you or yours.
We are just tired of being invisible.
Why? See above.
Black women are not to blame for every damn thing.
Just remember, she is you. You are her.
The next time you want to bash Black women as a
whole, call your mother first.
Say all of that to her, instead.
And still, we will march for you.
We will speak out against the murders of unarmed you.
We will continue sacrificing to raise you.
We will fight for you.
Black women and Gay Black men
Who love Blackness.
We will love you, Black man.
Always.

Divine Intervention

A paradigm shift is among us...

Human (r)Evolution

A paradigm shift is among us...

The day is coming for us
to break free of social constructs.
We've been pawns on a chessboard...
Living in a capitalistic society that spiritually,
we can't afford.
We're in an age of transformative change.
We outnumber the very few that we allow to rule us
Then we turn around and depend on them to school us
When everything you need to know
is already inside of you.
They want you to believe objects are everything...
That's why many willfully enslave themselves in debt.
But, if their education was
as important as they chop it up to be
then it'd be more affordable or free.
There is nothing you don't know that can't be learned.
Money only speaks because
we choose to know the language.
Millions of homeless people. Millions of empty places.
I can't be the only one who seeks to change this.
Pawns play a big role in a chess game
though they're often underestimated.
They're sacrificed to save the queen and king
but can become royalty when tensions are escalated.
People are comfortably blind and submissive
to the point that the idea of rebellion is scary.
And the rest are so complacent

they'll fight to stay oppressed.
Even with all the burdens they carry.
It's a slave cycle...
We awake everyday trying to make ends meet
in this rat race.
We take on so many bills to maintain a living.
Working 9 to 5s instead of living.
People don't even know about the play they're acting in.
The playwrights? They couldn't name half of them.
We work hard for not enough money
to pay for things we can't afford
then we just give their money back to them.
That's capitalism....
There's only one thing worse than nuclear weapons
and biological warfare.
When those who keep this country going
have to be on welfare
Because they've been deprived of food,
shelter, and healthcare.
We take so much for granted. Even air.
We are killing this planet and we don't care.
I mean, hey, we all have to die someday, right?
So, what's the use in putting up a fight?
Perhaps, because otherwise you only exist.
Why contribute to a system
that doesn't always give back to you?
If you really want to just not give a fuck...
Just know it's a snake before you pick it up.
If we all wake up tomorrow
and decide not to pay rent anymore
No one would be able to do a thing about it.

This is the world we live in.
And, history has shown that if you don't need it
you can live without it.
We've succumbed to infection
and our children need protection.
We stop the cycle by changing the way we think.
We've forgotten and we don't need books to remember
because our higher selves hold all the ink.
There is nothing you don't know
that can't be remembered.
Deception only speaks because
we choose to know the language.
Whether political, economic, or social. I'm hopeful...
But when we internalize is when we can change them.

Beyond race, we are all one mind
And, being mindful is where you begin.
Cause folks always focus on external (r)evolutions,
Yet, they forget about the (r)evolution within.

The Pseudo-Revolutionary

I yell out "Revolution!"
But I don't know what it truly means.
I've grown locs and I write about "The Struggle",
So, I must be a part of the team.
I've heard of Martin Luther King,
So, I'm only following his Dream.
I honor chicks with "nappy" hair
They're the only ones who are queens.
I've heard Bob Marley's music
So, I wear his shirts and smoke weed.
But who is this Haile Selassie figure, though?
How did he or she become Rasta creed?
I spend all my time on the internet
Blogging and bragging about my intellect.
I put my people down and call them coons,
My pretentiousness deserves respect.
I partied my way through college
And, I barely got by with Cs.
But I'm both smarter and better than you,
Since, I'm so informed with my several degrees.
I've read all about Huey P.
I know all about Angela Davis.
I've even met Nikki G.
I can quote phrases from all of their pages.
Black people embarrass me, sometimes.
Birds of the same feather don't flock together.
Yet, I spend more time
complaining about my community
Than I do trying to make it better.

I trust the media and authorities
For I truly have no grasp on politics.
But, it's pretty cool to think radically,
(I checked out that Malcolm X flick).
Corporate Blacks are all sellouts,
And, Gandhi taught me to calm my fury.
But "By any means necessary", of course
If it means a blue-eyed devil can get buried.
All my problems are the White man's fault.
He's the reason I have no interest in my worth.
So, I'll change it by sitting around
and complaining about it,
All while wearing a Che Guevara shirt.
College is the only way to knowledge
Don't ever give into the system.
It is all a part of the scheme
Cause I can ALWAYS play the victim.
I continue to push for equality
Although, the White man is a cancer.
To hell with Huey P.'s philosophies
I'm a New Age Black Panther.
It is really only fair,
That all men be seen as equal to women.
But if I hit my boyfriend and he hits me back
I'm sending that no good nigga to prison.
I believe that just because I sport the look,
And, just because I've read a few books...
That I can deem myself a part of "The Cause"...
With my political poetry and all.
I don't even know what "Black Power" means
But, I wear it because the shoes fit.

I don't truly honor or know my history...
But I'm still apart of the Afro-centric movement.
I say "NiggA" over "NiggER"
It's a common urban law.
But if a White man calls me a "Nigga"
I'll punch that nigga in his jaw.
In reality I point my fist to the sky
Because, I just want the attention.
While I'm up here thinking I'm so different,
I'm really just another statistic.
The word "revolutionary"
Is being watered down to the fullest.
What difference am I making, really?
I'm not even willing to take a bullet.

Parallels

Dear life...
I don't know what you want from me.
I cycle in and out like rentals
in my attempts to be transcendental.
I search for happiness as a tourist
wandering among a dark forest.
Parallel to line intervals...
I don't believe in Time.
I engineered these parallels...
Pushing envelopes and watching them bend.
Bending time and changing minds
as a means to continuum ends.
In a forest full of wolves and nightly creatures
that stalk me with no recollection.
Their existence is of persistence.
I feel Tempted. Defenseless.
But I salivate on a relentless pursuit
to conquer and understand.
Pushing boundaries all around me
in timeless parallelograms.
These two dimensions open portals
to where mere mortals never die.
I close my eyes to see the truth. (I don't believe in time.)

Tick... Tock... I don't believe in time.
We walk among paths from other paths
where jaded perceptions lead the Blind.
Tick... Tock... I don't believe in time.

Weakened vines grow from street signs
among unearthly concrete lines.

In this forest I can hear the whispers
from ghouls and ghosts of the night.
They cycle in and out like rentals
in their attempts to be confidential.
They shed secrets of the Sun
between moon shun parallels.
Surrounded by bark and limbs of the pompous...
I must now rely on my conscious.
Time after time I have defined time in mind
to press rewind and look behind.
I can now draw lines through time...
All while swinging on pendulums of the divine.
I taste free on the tip of my tongue,
with only the Moon to guide me.
I can feel the light inside me...
I never doubt the sunrise. This is only temporary...
My ancestors measured time by counting constellations
in their nightly observations.
I just need my space...
Through many dimensions of time and space.
Trying to find my place...
Between quantum quantified parallels.
Considering all I have faced I find faith in hyperspace
Where... mind supersedes matter.
(I don't believe in time.)
So if a tree falls in the forest
does it go on to make a sound?
My screams of silence go unheard so I...
stalk the ground.

Tick... Tock... I don't believe in time.
Wandering in and out of wooden acres,
where I am first to lead the line.
Tick... Tock... I don't believe in time.

Trusting intuition and superstition
for we design the mind.
Placebo effects of sunsets
allow me to create and innovate.
They cycle in and out like rentals
in my attempts to free my mental.
Separate my body from my mind.
Eye meditate to crescent moon sky.
Like a convalescent adolescent
now guided by their 3rd eye.
An inmate in a mental prison
where I had nothing but time...
To locate the patterns of Saturn
while swinging on pendulums of the divine.
Surrounded by branches and tree trunks
that seek to debunk my methods.
Without the time to limit myself to time...
Still, I seek and feel the message.
The thickness of this forest
has no bearing on me while in orbit.
In periods and moments of an instant...
These wolves remain to be persistent.
I have learned to take my time
from many roads now intertwined.
Paths aligned and struggles combined...
(I don't believe in time.)

Tick... Tock... I don't believe in time.
Expect the unexpected. Forests universally decline.
Tick... Tock... I don't believe in time.

Like forest fires and endless desires,
I redesign then free my mind.

So, meet me at the parallels of dominion
where egos go silent and suns have risen.
Where love begins its course
to show us the source of all that is pure and true.
Meet me between the worlds
of star-relative motioned planets.
Where we are products of space-time...
Free from the grievance of parallegiance.
Meet me in yesterday,
moving counterclockwise to understand the future.
Where the second hand on watch
bands distorts and alters life spans.
Meet me at the event horizon
of time warps and relative wormholes.
Where grandfather clocks can only watch
the ticks and tocks of life's Sequence.
Meet me at the water,
where these forests end and parallels begin.
Where the tools used to measure time
are not subject to the human mind.
Meet me at the parallels...
Where consciousness exists in multiple realities.
Where we can defy the laws of physics
and literally float on cloud nine.

Tick... Tock... I don't believe in time.
Mentally I travel at the speed of light,
theoretically stringed to the divine.
Tick... Tock... I don't believe in time.
So, meet at the parallels
where the limits of time are redefined.
Free your mind.

Mindful Eating

About two years ago I set out on a journey
to better my health.
I cut out dairy, junk food and soda.
Began exercising to better myself.
Yet when I visit my parents it's so hard to say the words
"I'm vegan".
It still takes some believing on my own quest
to make odds even.
My father refuses to take me seriously,
my mother just looks at me curiously...
I get made fun of,
coming from a family where there's only one of me.
I grew up surrounded by liquor and cigarettes.
Eating healthy wasn't allowed.
My father even jokes and claims
you can bury him with a cow.
But between hormones and pesticides,
I've learned it'd be best if I...
Ate organic fruits, grains, and vegetables
and simply set the rest aside.
But I must testify...
I was raised on soul food.
It's hard to go from shopping at Moo and Oink
to spending more money at Whole Foods.
But as a Black being from Black culture I
have come to better fathom my history.
With a little research you'll find most things you
consume here are a mystery.
Your government is systematically killing you
and has the nerve to be billing you...
And, on what grounds?
That they're supposed to be for the people??

In slavery days our masters would eat good...
Only leaving us scraps to eat
in which we did the best we could.
That's how chitterlings and pig feet
came to be part of our diet.
I used to love to dig in beef
til' I saw the best killers are quiet.
As good as soul food tastes,
we just fill ourselves with fat and grease.
We're basically eating nothing and this is what leaves
Blacks deceased.
We struggle with high blood pressure,
cholesterol, heart disease and diabetes...
Yet, most people will look at you like you're crazy
if you hand them a plate that isn't meaty.
I mean, I know it's not necessarily true
that you're unhealthy if you eat meat.
We all have our guilty pleasures
and salmon is a secret I can't keep.
Eggs are hard to write off my checklist
For they're an essential part of my breakfast.
I have moments of weakness with butterfingers
and those damned oatmeal creampies.
But every time I give in I realize
it's like saying "F--k the truth."
I know this stuff is bad for me
and I am aware there are substitutes.
The point is, I'm working on it. I'm along on this
journey, too.
I'm becoming mindful of what I consume
and reading ingredients should worry you.
High fructose corn syrup is in everything
and tends to haunt my favorite treats.
You are what you eat

and some of us are willfully ignorant to sweets.
So, through fasting and purification
I built a relationship with my foods.
It's like a lasting meditation
for what you eat even affects your moods.
Where I grew up there are fast food restaurants
and low-end grocery stores on every street.
Did you know McDonald's feeds you plastic
and Burger King uses horse meat?
No coincidence the shittiest food chains are in poor,
Black neighborhoods.
Thank your government.
(You gotta pay to eat right when in that "street life").
Even going to a barbecue is hard to do...
When you live in a nation where certain traditions
have become a part of you.
But choosing vegan bars over Snicker's bars
is something I simply had to do...
Cause 9 times out of 10, if it's advertised on t.v.
it's bad for you.
Be you vegetarian or omnivore,
what you eat will come out of your pores.
Even vegans have to be careful
of the amount of soy they consume.
Some things are okay in moderation,
just don't always give in to temptations.
For most bad things are designed
to make you crave it all the time.
If we can truly take the time and learn
to grow and prepare food ourselves.
No longer will we take for granted
all it takes to get it on our shelves.
We must feed our babies and teach them
to be mindful of their paths.
Take care of your vessel. It's the only one you have.

<u>3rd Eye</u>

Sometimes, it is hard to fathom
that I am composed of merely atoms.
Therefore, the laws of physics
tend to override my flaws and critics.
I am inspired by tires that barrel down
the roads of freedom.
But where are these roads supposed to be
when freedom ain't free?
So, I look to science for compliance...
I lacked hunger when I was younger
but now I can't help but feel like I haven't eaten in years.
Cause my spirit is hungry
and it wasn't long before I got the hint.
I was an aeroplane on descent
'til I came to question man's intent.
History is told through the eyes of the victor,
yet I believed it all cause it's in print.
As I clung to material possessions
that man has taken it upon himself to invent.
I have always loved to study
Isaac Newton and Huey Newton.
They both developed a full understanding
of the forces that hold us down.
Gravity. An unknown travesty at the hands of man.
And, only a few can see through
from 3rd eyes and pineal glands.
To reach my mind liberation
I suffered through mind gentrification.
Yet I'm surrounded by all who are indifferent
about being a cause for resistance.
To be a cause for resistance
I learned the laws of physics...

Since you can't fight the forces
that be unless you first look within thee.
We are being lied to.
And we're being fed so many illusions...
To the point that my perception
was unable to see the deception.
They took the Sun from my sky
as I wandered aimlessly through their night.
Til I got my night vision goggles,
otherwise known as 3rd eye sight.
I didn't think I was being controlled.
I didn't believe in the illuminati.
Until I took time to look into all the poison
I have mindlessly put into my body.
So I asked myself "Are you paying attention?
Or do you simply accept all that is given?"
We're in a political and educational prison
and being divided among our religions.
"Do you believe that money reflects on your purpose?
And what you drive makes you perfect?
Are you willing to dig yourself in debt since
without a degree they say you're worthless?
Wake up from this shit, J.
Think for yourself. Question authority."
It saddened me that my material greed
had superseded my spiritual needs.
Through meditation and preservation
I decided to look within me.
And now I find myself floating on air
as I resist the forces that be.
So, can you stomach the weightlessness?
Can you rise above all you're confined to?
Will there ever come a day we all realize
bank accounts don't define you?

We come from the Universe.
So, I look to science for compliance.
I have come to master zero gravity
as it transcends man and his travesty.
Cause it's about time. No, this is really about "time".
How much longer can we go before
we are no longer comfortably blind?
Stop searching for validation through I-phones,
Facebook, and cars.
You want to know what you are?
Step outside and thank the stars.
Our relevance is in the elements...
Not through resume's and television.
So, elevate. Levitate.
Celebrate your spirit through 3rd eye vision.
I'm just feeding my hungers,
you don't have to agree with my complaints.
I just wanted to share my joy
in that I no longer limit myself to man's constraints.
So, don't be afraid to let go and face yourself.
Don't be afraid of what you will find.
Play the game if you have to,
but don't let them chain a free mind.
Through my 3rd eye I see Rebellion.
I see freedom. I see truth.
A shift is among us for, through my 3rd eye I see you.
Freedom ain't free unless it starts within thee.
There's a reason why astronauts
are so good at what they do.

Cliché Revolutionary Piece

If you cut the head off the body will fall.
To get inside the head you must first become the body.
Your politicians all play for the same team.
They just find very different ways to say the same thing.
Soldiers have shed blood
for those that wish to keep their hands clean.
It's such a beautiful tragedy.
Cause, there were sacrifices made
so the rich can continue to get paid.
And, I may make mistakes but I never make them twice.
They say if you can't find something to live for
then find something to die for.
The makings of revolutionary thinking.
They'll kill everything that matters
in terms of difference.
The prime of our existence
has been designed to make us victims.
We depend so much on a corrupted system.
They make you think joining the military
makes you a revolutionary.
But that couldn't be further from the truth.
You'll be a part of something other than,
but not greater than yourself.
Remember,
not everyone that looks like a sheep is a sheep.
It's just that when you meet people where they are,
the truth is easier to seek.
And, their secrets become harder for them to keep.
They will do anything to keep us divided.
So, do we unite so we can fight it
or simply go along despite it?
The menu is one sided...

And, we continue to eat even if lies are today's special.
Our voices are now whispers
being plucked away like whiskers.
While our leaders sip champagne
after a successful campaign.
Before action must be awakening.
So I've spent time in observation...
To watch....
As they close our borders,
ignoring that their own immigration
Was the birth of a nation.
I watch...
As they forced us to follow their God
and read their book
while they chip away at our history like crooks.
I watch...
Television and the internet because if I am distracted
They will assume I'll forget.
I watch...
As the notoriety of secret societies
and the financially elite
construct tunnels beneath our very feet.
I watch...
As we justify wars
because we can't keep a score
of how many countries now hate us.
I watch...
As those who scored well on the ASVAB
got sent to Baghdad where they bag dads.
I watch...
Cause, my sight is all I have and nothing will add up
if you learn to do the math.
So, I watch...
People looking down into their I-phones,
too distracted to look up and see the drones.

I watch...
As real housewives of Atlanta and Facebook
keeps our faces out of books.
Cause, I refuse to avoid the truth.
I have nieces and nephews.
I am concerned about our youth.
It is easy to lose hope in humanity
when you're American and
everyone around you is perishing.
Cause liberals are miserable and rich republicans
are doubling their bank accounts.
This is only a small amount of the issues at hand.
In the grand scheme of things
they all play for the same team so...
Take a minute to ask yourself who you're voting for.
What contributions have you made to the constitution?
There are still people walking this planet,
suffering from atom bomb pollution.
The signs are everywhere. Are you paying attention?
Are you so blind to defend them
or are you apart of the resistance?
They think they've deceived me
and now they are coming for you.
So, tell me what are you going to
do when you wake up, too?

Let's stop watching and start doing.

<u>The Homeful Man</u>

I saw a homeless man today.

He was staring off into the Sun.

As if the sky was his roof.

As if he knew where he is from.

Reminding me he was not homeless

But, homeful.

Black Questions

We are taught to believe we come from nothing...
That we are animals with low IQs.
That our brown skin is dark and disgusting.
We are single mothers and baby mamas.
Violent and always in drama.
We are thieves, thugs, and crooks and
couldn't be paid to read a book.
If we're not hated, we're tolerated.
If not in a cell, we must have made bail.
Even in college we still fail
cause they say beyond that we don't excel.
It's not enough to think like them.
(Weaves, blue contacts and fake nails).
Cause to be Black in America
means to lose so much of yourself.
I'm from a city where young Black men
are currently playing Blackjack...
You're considered lucky if you make it to 21.
We're unappreciative of our mothers.
Deny our sisters. Kill our brothers.
We've been taught to hate ourselves,
to deceive and berate one another.
Dark skin vs light skin. Permed hair vs natural hair.
Field niggas vs House niggas.
Separation is our dilemma.
How can we rid ourselves of thorns
if the roots are deeply planted in concrete?
Where do the lines between blaming them
and taking our own responsibility meet?
We think our questions have been answered,
but so many answers are being questioned.
We're collectively fighting a cancer
that we've been tricked to see as a blessing.

Freedom. Do you really think we all have it?
We're game among this game and they're the hunters.
You're the rabbit.
They run this like a track meet so,
the only way out is to be an athlete.
Believe it or not, you're still a slave.
Even if you're among the Black elite.
How can there ever be unity
if we are greatly lacking of community?
Let's talk about these things
while we still have the opportunity...
What is a good way to control a race?
I ask myself what would I do.
I would capture you and set standards.
Let the truth get by you.
I would lie to you and steal your history.
Do all I can to defy you.
Then teach you to hate each other
and multiply that by two.
I don't care whether or not
the letter Willie Lynch wrote is true.
We can't start businesses in our own neighborhoods.
That alone should speak to you.
Were we the first astronomers and philosophers?
Were we kings and queens for thousands of years?
Was 400 years of slavery all it took
to turn Blacks against their peers?
If stereotypes represent truths
then what does that say about our roots?
Why do we idolize the worst rappers
and treat our women like prostitutes?
Who is really to blame for the state of hip hop?
And, why did we mourn Paul Walker's death
more than Nelson Mandela's?

Why do some White people think we have the same,
if not more opportunities?
And, that when we purposely create things
for ourselves it's called "reverse racism"?
How can we be racist in a hegemonic society
where we are simply reacting
to standards set not to benefit us?
Why won't statistics show
there are more Black men in college than jail?
Why do we praise a White Jesus
in matters of heaven and hell?
Why are misguided Black men
given ultimatums by the judge?
So, to avoid jail and intervene
you have to join the Marines?
Are Black men fighting for their country
or fighting their country?
The government is supposed to protect them
yet allows their communities to sink.
Why does the prison industrial complex
just happen to exist?
While keeping Black men in jail
and keeping rich White men rich?
I remember a time in history
that you couldn't run fathers away...
So...
Why are so many Black households
lacking fathers today?
Why are we as prone to mug shots
as we are to blood clots?
Why don't Black men and Black women
love one another anymore?

What is the point of reading books
if you skip over the contents?
What is the point of having thoughts
if you're unaware you're even conscious?
How can we rid ourselves of thorns
if the roots are deeply planted in concrete?
Where does the line between blaming their norms
and taking our own responsibility meet?
I know what you're thinking.
Another Black conscious poet complaining
about problems with her race
and talking that revolution shit, right?
Nah. We're all on a journey of believers...
Cause, having locs and wearing dashikis
doesn't mean you have it all figured out, either.
In all honesty, fuck race. It's an illusion. A distraction.
With answers to these questions
we'll all tune into that's really happening.
Cause, that's the point.
To see everything as polarized.
Unable to see our duality as one working in harmony.
I know it's hard to ignore racial issues
when you're living in America.
I know it's hard to move beyond the past
when pain is so deeply rooted in our character.
But, if you live and question nothing,
chances are you're not in the right business.
Cause truth is, we're all slaves...
Even those with white privilege.
The powers that be have tricked us
into seeing things in terms of competition...
We don't see how everything points back to money
cause we're so caught up in racial tension.
I don't need to be a theorist to see a conspiracy.

There's a reason that for me to tackle chains
I first have to tackle fear in me.
Your leaders are not leaders
but I won't say names or place blame.
Some of you voted for him but they ALL deal in disdain.
It is much bigger than who you vote for.
This is economic warfare.
We are spiritual beings being limited by physical means.
I don't proclaim to have the answers.
I just know America needs a movement.
Blacks and Whites finding solutions
for even teachers are still students.
Fighting the real enemy first begins in our communities.
Fix the problems. Tackle the questions.
Rise above and change our perceptions.

Remember Love

The world is a puzzle.
There's no need to make sense of it.
Everything is everything.
We just have to live to our benefit.
All that is important lies beyond questions and names.
We roll with the punches and find lessons in pain.
Some people never know what it is or what it was.
No surprise there are those who don't know how to hug.
It seems we're sent to school
to learn everything, except how to love.
I'm not saying skip school.
Just be aware of what you're going for.
Outside of the classroom
there's much more to be explored...
We're swimming toward happiness
in a cesspool of hate.
So, just look to the sky
for things you can neither confirm nor deny.
We try to reach the shore and do something
as simple as keep food on our plates.
And, in between trying to find balance in both
We've completely forgotten what we need most.
The answer to conflict is not always war,
But if you see it as an option
it's the first thing you'll resort to.
We create all these reasons
as to why countries have wronged us
Then fight over territories that don't belong to us.
But a distracted heart should dull your sword.
And rightfully so...
Cause falling on your own sword
is like your mind writing a check your heart can't afford.
We must re-label, reattribute,

refocus, revalue, and restore.
We exist in one of many nine dimensions.
What string theorists define
as the lines between the sky and divine intervention.
Where I say "Namaste and Ashé" with divine intentions.
Now is the most precious time of all...
We have to understand that world poverty
and spiritual poverty go hand in hand...
And, in between trying to find balance in both
We've completely forgotten what we need most.
The most important questions
cannot be answered by books, experts, or systems.
Success is knowing your purpose
and moving forward with it accordingly.
Life is priceless so be whoever you can afford to be.
The schemes of regimes are not made to last.
Even the stars are born and disappear...
Cause harmony in the selective
creates harmony in the collective.
You are your own cosmic engineer.
Whether or not you have a proper teacher
depends on what you wish you to learn.
The rotation of Sirius B and Sirius A
is the exact same pattern as DNA.
Ego will make you believe
we are all separate and incomplete.
But you are interconnected by the flower of life.
It is important to live in love and be free.
For, in the balance of both,
We can begin to remember what we need most.
Provide service. Accumulate good will.
Forgive and forget.
Rise above the ego and live in abundance.
Anything else you do will just become redundant.
Remember the love.

Time Traveler

Instead of paying thousands for professors to talk of it
I now acquire knowledge of the path by walking it.
On NY buses and trains,
I'd sit and watch the people change.
Spent good time in lecture halls
but learned more by boarding planes.
I embraced the unknown
to discover anywhere I go is home...
And, I come from so much more than just Chicago.
Eye am as open as Eye've ever been
as a traveling artist...
For knowledge of self is knowledge of the cosmos.
I left the emptiness of violence
in full bloom and loud bars,
Finding emptiness and silence
under full moons and loud stars.
Hiked many Mt. Rainiers,
Strolled Canadian beaches and piers...
I'm a Nomad with no cash, living like she has no past.
Marking footprints on many soils
for past and future reference.
For, time is of the essence
and my mind is the in the present.
They say if you don't leave you won't arrive
And, travel gives all I need to feel alive.
All land belongs to us humans, beneath the surface.
So, explore this planet, for it is a part of your
purpose.

$E = mc^2$

As we transcend through life's seasons...
I overstand sometimes you have to do wrong
for all the right reasons.
If nothing exists entirely alone,
then we're all chasing after the unknown.
I'm somewhere between Marcus Garvey
and Terrence McKenna...
With a little mix of a Chicago Winter.
Getting my grind on in different time zones.
I am equal to pure energy. All these MCs squared.
I am everywhere and nowhere
both right at the same time.
Sometimes I feel I'm in way too deep.
The water rises well beyond my feet.
But I am allowed to be flawed and make mistakes.
Interesting how fate rhymes with the word faith.
I'm from where they leave shells on niggas backs
like Raphael and Donatello.
Where the faces of poverty haunt the projects
like Candyman.
That's just some shit you'd have to witness
to understand.
Where no adult males are around
to teach a boy to be a man.
Where niggas kill each other over someone else's land.
Where water of life gets lost in the sand...
Where Love's lost in the
imbalance of supply and demand.
What shall nourish me will destroy me.
This is a matter of life and death.
They say how you feel influences
your perception of the world
And, most don't know their right from left.

I write from the depths of human consciousness
No need for psychedelics. Cause DMT already be in me.
And, we be free.
Cause what I see from most people I see in me.
I get at these niggas with spiritual theory.
A metaphysical Einstein.
Cherishing my history like fine wine.
The type of shit you'd never find on primetime.
But it doesn't matter.
Cause, their manipulation is no stipulation to the facts.
You come from Suns laced on the universe's back.
So, if I say you have star qualities
it now means more than ever.
I find my truth in stormy weather.
The best thing I have come to know
is that I know absolutely nothing.
The point is to keep ascending
for we mystics are not perfect.
Any second of the journey is worth it.
Everything is temporary. Even you.
All is supposed to be in the moment that it is.
You'll make better choices
when you realize you only have this moment to live.
I don't have another moment
to give backward movements.
I'm pushing forward with room for improvements.
I swear to God I've almost tapped out.
Then I considered how my mom took it
when my grandmother died.
Had a nigga thinking otherwise.
She often visits me from the other side
With the same look on her face
I see when I look into my mother's eyes.
She speaks to me with the voice of a martyr
Cause fucking with me is like fucking with her daughter.

And, I don't care what the mass depicts.
The media is a lie.
Look closely and you'll see clearly through half the shit.
I rise above the greed and take ego trips
with destination not guaranteed.
Cause I'm from where they leave shells on niggas backs
like Raphael and Donatello.
Where the faces of poverty haunt the projects
like Candyman.
That's just some shit you'd have to witness
to understand.
Where no adult males are around
to teach a boy to be a man.
Where niggas kill each other over someone else's land.
Where water of life gets lost in the sand.
Where Love's lost in the
imbalance of supply and demand.

If I die tomorrow,
I will be alive and well in the hearts of many.
When I leave here you'll remember
all I've achieved here.

I am equal to pure energy.

Freedom of Choice

Love inspires.
Love evolves.
Love teaches.
Love hurts.
Love heals.
Love transcends.
Love frees.
Love bends.
Transcending above and beyond.
Spread all among the Universe.
Love is everything and so are you.
Choose Love.

Commitment

I am committed to Liberatory Learning.
Paving paths toward Liberatory earning.
We have all the tools. They need them.
We can define our freedom.
We were planting seeds well before the Garden of Eden.
There are streets in need of healing.
While in process of rebuilding
We give way to the future. Yielding.
I want to facilitate a space of blackness.
Help folks replace their anger with Love and action.
Make way for young talented authors,
Help them locate all within to Foster
A paradigm shifting curriculum of color.
The backbone of a system that works against us.
So this is for us by us and with us.
Fists up.
Let's discuss.

A Letter to the Future

Dear Future,

This is the past speaking to you.
From beyond the grave I am reaching to you.
Every time you speak we are speaking through you.
We stay alive, breathing through you.
Don't let them keep you from doing you.
Do not cooperate in however you operate.
Whatever space and time you populate.
Continue to postulate our burdens
we all carry on shoulders until you feel safe enough
to say you've lost the weight.
There is no other way, until this system ceases
to see another day. Infiltrate. Mark the dates.
This is fate. Leave secret codes to their gates
for those who come after you. You are chapter two.
We must keep going. We must keep knowing.
The ties and layers here are deep flowing.
You come from us. You come from dust off the stars.
You must know whom you are... for us to survive.
Thrive. Drive. Stay alive. Dive. Strive. Leave and arrive.
You are the successor for our fight
against the oppressor. Lift us far.
Past future and present... You are a gift.
Remember these words
and give your own to each sentence.
Then pass it along to your own descendants.

You are our wildest dreams.

Rose. Thorn.

We say all is about equity

But poverty is the trajectory

It's like we are all cooking in the same kitchen

Yet only a few have the recipes.

So, if you can't stand the heat

You have freedom to build your own stove.

The actualism of capitalism.

All the ugly thorns of a beautiful rose.

Plant your seeds.

Panther

Everything is made of light, including matter,
and without matter there would be no sound.
Atoms and planets arrange themselves
in geometrical patterns. All Around.
Patterns = father. Nature = Mother.
"Om Mani Padme Hum".
Cosmology can be guided by science,
religion, or metaphysics of the moon.
Stars appear to be stationary
because of how distant they are.
And, if it's any constellation to life's complications
I have died 1000 times, but I'm here.
Reflecting the light of being conscious
of my consciousness.
The Grand Unified Theory will help to integrate
all the known laws of physics.
Perhaps, bringing together relativity
and quantum mechanics.
Yet you and I are being held down by a singularity.
Our light cannot escape.
But singularities are points where properties
are infinite and this Love is all on Faith.
Everyone wants to be Malcolm
or Huey P. Newton these days
but scatter when oppression begins shooting.
See, I'm a Black Panther for matters of the heart.
Armed with rose-colored bullets in self-defense
of patriarchal, systematic tyranny.
We connect in spirit. We connect in science.
Transcending man...
Breaking hearts and awakening the art within us all.
The Universe will manifest what it manifests.
For it is Love in all of its fights,
And the Universe in me will never rest.

<u>We Be</u>

We be reflections of Divine human connection.
We be a collection of everyone else's introspections.
We be our mothers hard work.
Our grandmothers yard work.
We be our fathers golden skin.
Our grandfathers' golden kin.
We be spirit in the flesh.
Spiritual beings and freedom fighters.
We be providers and night riders.
The resistance. Outsiders.
We be the resilience underneath our ancestor's feet.
We be Chicago. These... Southside, outside streets.
We be from generations of both slave and king DNA.
Paved the way to lead today.
We make beds where freedom lay.
We be creative. We be with blood of the Natives.
We be revolutionaries and activists.
Taking on pain like masochists.
We be with bloodlines of Shamans and Choctaw.
...Peaceful and hostile.
We be strangers in Moscow.
We be paradigms and mystics.
We be dreamers yet realistic.
We be time travelers and rhyme battlers.
Both Artistic and Futuristic.
We be mercury retrogrades and refracting telescopes.
We be ...Space-time continuums.
We be hella dope to hella folks.
We be mathematics and athletic.
We be scientists and vinylists.
We be queers and engineers.
Survivalists and tribalists.
We be from them slums.
Where... we match heartbeats to drums.
We be Sun reflectors and child protectors.
Where fathers leave after they cum.
We be Maya Angelou and Marcus Garvey.

We be Huey Newton and Rita Marley.
We be like... Lines of rich white coke,
to these entitled rich white folk.
We be Malcolm X and Lao Tzu.
We be everything without you.
We be the ones they imitate
but just can't seem to outdo.
We be buried, unpolished diamonds.
We be unknowns. Misunderstood.
We be the inner-city violence.
We be roots of a forest's wood.
We be the least beautiful. We be the most beautiful.
We be the ones who never die.
The African proverb of a funeral.
We be third eye pineal glands and all of the 7 chakras.
We be from Africa and Jamaica.
We be Einsteins and young doctors.
We be from burned crosses and nooses.
We be Sun Tzu and Confucius.
We be harmonious and Infinite.
Yet we intelligent and ruthless.
We be hip hop. We be global now.
We be millionaires and moguls now.
We be of a hood mentality mixed in with spirituality.
We be rebellion. We be aliens.
We be women and men of our prayers.
We be what our ancestors could never imagine.
We flat tired with plenty spares.
We be this.
We be that.
We be FREE.
We be Black.
We are the history being repeated.
We be ...Undefeated.

Descent
&
Ascension

The Life
&
Death Continuum

I was born at Michael Reese and raised on Peoria street

Chicago Sky

I was born at Michael Reese and raised on Peoria street
Where I first planted my feet on rough concrete.
Right off of 81st and Halsted.
My mother would come home, exhausted.
Car won't start and windows frosted...
The streets were cold with politicians even colder.
Every day she walked those streets
Delivering mail so we could eat.
Climbing through 12 inches of snow
to sweating in blistering heat.
Where my father did construction
among the city's corruption.
Did you witness a crime? Say nothing.
Though I had to leave her to explore the world
She still stays in the back of my mind.
Kanye asked if he could come home again
And, these days I understand why.
Memories of walking the magnificent mile.
From the watchtower to Wrigley Field
--this place is versatile.
Having lunch at the Grande Lux Cafe downtown.
Cruising to the sounds...of Common Sense and Lupe.
Thankful for the chance to wake up to a new day.
Walks along Lake Michigan... Listening
To Do or Die, Twista and Psychodrama
Through the streets of Hyde Park, home to the Obamas.
Where Blacks and Whites have different perceptions
Of the city and its direction.
When the Sun sets you can see the rise
of fog from ashore.
Nighttime is the right time to see
what the guides hide on those tours.
The Moon brings the goons
out from behind their destiny.
Sometimes you can only watch helplessly.
You're safer near Millenium Park after Dark.
You're in the clear near Navy Pier.

But, there's no overcoming on Martin Luther King Drive.
Where the most segregated city leaves many deprived.
At the Taste of Chicago you'll take a bite of deep dish.
But, this food for thought shields the city's secrets.
We went from doing the super bowl shuffle
To counting bodies wrapped in duffle bags.
(And, we've yet to take out the trash...)
All these bodies in Lake Michigan
Post-Slavery, we still don't know how to swim.
But we gather for BBQ
and good times at Rainbow Beach.
Despite politicians and police,
the biggest gang in these streets.
The South Side...
Where the committee has no pity on children of the city.
The streets are full but schools and libraries are empty.
Mothers and ghosts of fathers
are crying while their sons are dying.
Stray bullets will catch you slippin' on the Dan Ryan.
In this stop and go traffic
We still get Vice Lords and Gangster's Disciples.
With a history having changed
from the time of Larry Hoover.
As a child I was taught to fear bullets,
not Michael Myers or Freddy Krueger.
Englewood, where many are living reckless.
Where they kill their own brothers,
using all but their mind as a weapon.
Where we're growing and dying
from roots and seeds of propaganda.
Where police just shoot
without tazing or stating Mirandas.
When I see those skyscrapers and that Chicago River
I'm reminded that I survived these Chicago winters.
With memories of walking the magnificent mile.
Where being a Bears, Bulls, and Cubs fan
never goes out of style.
Having lunch at the Grande Lux Cafe downtown.

Cruising to the sounds of...
Smashing Pumpkins and Lupe.
Thankful for the chance to wake up to a new day.
Walks along Lake Michigan...
Listening to Do or Die, Twista and Psychodrama
Through the streets of Hyde Park, home to the Obamas.
Where Blacks and Whites have different perceptions
Of the city and its progression.
When the sunsets you can see
the rise of fog from ashore.
Nighttime is the right time to see
what the guides hide on those tours.
The dimmed Stars come out,
not knowing their own allure.
The Moon brings these goons
out from behind their destiny.
Until they come to rest in peace...
in a morgue at Michael Reese.
No longer planting their feet on such rough concrete.

<u>Downward Spiral</u>

I knew a boy named Victor.

He couldn't hold his liquor.

He always drank away

His sorrows and dismay.

He never had a shoulder.

He got it from his mother.

Another faceless soldier

Spending useless time

Fighting his own mind.

He got it from his mother

He never wore a rubber.

He swallowed under covers.

An undercover brother

Where he succumbed to others

From undercover lovers.

He tried to study business

But failed to grasp the physics

Of gravity.

<u>Grandfather Moon</u>

We suffer more through imagination
than we do in reality.
So, to change your views
you must change your mentality.
And, through endless possibilities we're all here...
Held in spiral arms of the Milky Way galaxy.
I miss waking up at the crack of dawn
Seeing you headed out to walk a mile.
Reading the newspaper and eating fruit.
Greeting me with a bright-eyed smile.
I cannot stand Milky Way bars
But I loved them when you gave them to me.
You had an endless amount of peppermints
And, managed to always save some for me.
Yet, I'm not quite sure how I'll continue to visit
Houston without the joy of embracing you.
There is no sure thing but death.
Life has awakened you to that naked truth.
It is the one thing with no bias...
Taking you in strength or in weakness.
I live in reality that death is no secret
And, I imagine you're somewhere peace is.
Whenever we lose someone
There are things we feel we have to know.
So, with a heavy heart I breathe in grief
Exhaling the acceptance of letting go.
'Cause, life is to be celebrated
From your first steps to your last breath.
Even well beyond the unexplainable

For if life is poetry, then so is death.
So, I write for you, Grandfather.
You've whispered much wisdom to my ears.
I think of you when I see my father's hands
It is through him that you are still here.
I've learned no one ever truly dies
But, we all tend to live in that fear.
You're alive in nature. You're alive in us.
And, that connection is quite clear.
So when I view trees, mountains, and night skies
I see you as one in the same.
You have returned from which you came.
And, you are everything, again.
Thank you for the memories grandfather
I wish you well on your transition.
I hope that wherever you are, you're laughing...
And, there are baseball games and plenty of fishing.
There are so many questions I'd like to ask you
While in this night in search of your light.
But, it's like questioning why the moon shines
When all that matters is that it's bright.

(*For my late grandfather, Joseph F. Roberts*)

Grandmother (Maternal)

When I was 9, I remember my mother loading the car.
And, if I knew it was the last time I'd see you
I'd have held you tighter.
I was too busy being a kid to pay attention.
And, I was too young to understand you were a fighter.
You were quite a woman and you'd hardly ever speak.
But I remember the tears that ran down your cheeks.
As, we pulled off headed back to our lives,
My siblings and I along for the drive.
My memories of Yazoo City are little to none
And images of you in my head are quite vague.
But I appreciate the times you've visited me since,
Teaching me more about you from beyond the grave.
I receive and know I'm a product of you
And, I am sure there is much more you wanted to do,
But I find peace whenever you take the time to speak
Saying "I love you and take care of your mother for me".

(For my late grandmother, Hattie Story)

<u>**Grandmother (Paternal)**</u>

It's been hard watching you grow old.
I see the pain you feel since Granddad left.
I doubt anyone misses him as much as you.
After 50 years I can't imagine how you'd readjust.
Your wisdom has always spoken volumes to me.
I miss eating your banana pudding and cake batter.
I like that I can talk to you about anything.
At times your ears are all that matters.
You and granddad always had interesting stories.
Believe it or not, I miss sitting with you in church.
You'd praise God in all his glory
And, showed me what it means to truly serve.
But I've had my own path to walk
And, your love for me has never been in question.
For a grandmother's love is open and honest
And, I thank you for your acceptance.

(*For my grandmother, Annie Roberts*)

Houseless

To the homeless man that froze to death:

I know I don't know you but I apologize.
I'm sure there were many times
you had to swallow pride.
Whatever the gray skies that led to your demise
I admit I'm among those
that wouldn't look you in the eye.
Growing up I was taught you all were failures.
Lazy bums with liquor bottles and drug paraphernalia.
I walk pass you in clean clothes
that have been tailored...
Hiding in drowning seas as an undercover sailor.
Trying to gain my sea legs
in these rough waters called the system...
For we're all one bad decision away from treading it.
Many are homeless
despite their homes, jobs, and outfits.
So, over time I've come to prefer the term "houseless".
Many will perish after
and many have perished before you.
Interestingly enough, I've been houseless before, too.
Despite my working efforts,
I know what it is like not to have...
Food, a bed, friends, or water for a bath.
At times it can terrifying
'til you're no longer scared of dying.
But, it reminded me of what's important
and was clarifying.
If "houselessness" is a choice, I am not sorry it has to be.
Quitting the rat race is priceless
and you should do that for free.
I find it moving how those with less
have so much more to give.
The same way people who are dying
try so much more to live.
Yet, we never question why poverty is even allowed.

While we float on false illusions of our money clouds.
So, I'm sorry for those who judged
and hesitated to love you.
I'm sorry for those who think they are above you.
I apologize for those too into their phones
and TV screens.
Addicted to alcohol, celebrity gossip,
fast food and caffeine.
We're lost. And we've lost our means to facilitate...
Boats and ships for all swimmers
with the rise of real estate.
I'm sorry for those
that don't think you worked hard enough.
Pointing fingers with dirty hands
like you're not a part of us.
I'm sorry you have to escape with that liquid sedative.
But we're all drunk on success--out of touch
and too competitive.
Hamsters on the wheel of false hope and Capitalism.
Taking mental hand-me-downs
from our mothers and fathers...
Who only want lives best
for their sons and their daughters.
So, they teach us to cooperate and sail smooth waters.
And, as long we learn to swim we can't do much harm.
But what good is swimming if you lose your arms?
So, I'm sorry you don't have a right
to food, clothing, and shelter.
For, there are those who lack compassion
and refuse to be helpers.
We think apathy and Darwinism are synonymous.
I'm sorry that to us you are anonymous.
I'm sorry that there are millions of bank owned homes
Empty and just sitting there,
yet too expensive for you to own.
We base our success
on how much more we have than the next.

We look down on choices
of those living paycheck to paycheck.
'Cause, we chase the dream
that we can all be millionaires
When this system is designed
to keep many of us in despair.
We are trillions in debt and it is mostly due to war.
Wars veterans like you fought in just to end up poor.
If I could I'd spread the wealth
and address your mental health.
But I barely make rent and can hardly take care of Self.
One can have a roof over their heart
with no lights, beds, or couches.
And, I consider these things
when I use the term "houseless".
I will share this poem in awareness,
that of us you are an extension.
Hoping that many others and myself
will take the time to pay you attention.
I'm sorry I misinterpreted
Darwin's "survival of the fittest".
It's about Love and adaptation.
Not who is strong and who isn't.
We made ships to smooth the experience
of Life's rough seas.
And, sailors like others and myself
are still searching for a breeze.
Here you are trying to swim
with no limbs or land to sail to.

You didn't fail society. Society failed you.

<u>For Kiana</u>

To parents a child is the greatest thing.
It changes you. It changes things.
It reminds you what is most important.
A reality check but a way to dream.
Like a much needed self expression
Giving you range as a way to sing.
It creates words for a silenced poet...
Or in life's film...The best rated scene.
It brings light from the darkness
And, gives one a sense of purpose.
Of all mistakes I have made
Here I have created something perfect.
The first time I held you in my arms
I then understood Love, completely.
I knew I'd have to be strong for you
And not let this world defeat me.
You went from walking and now to talking.
Teaching me things I have ever known.
Buying you new clothes every 6 months.
I cannot believe how much you've grown.
And, you will only continue to...
For, one day you'll look me eye to eye.
One day you'll go away to college
And, I'll be forced to say bye to my...
Fear. The fear I have of letting you go.
Knowing I raised a good human being.
And, here I am letting you know.
Of all disagreements to come
Of all times you'll feel misunderstood.
Just pay attention to the lessons
For all in life unfolds as it should.
As your parent you may come to doubt me.
I know we will both make mistakes.
Remember Love is always on time
And, forgiveness is never too late.
For, to parent a child is the greatest thing.
It changes you. It changes things.
It reminds you what is most important.
A reality check but a way to dream.

Library

All books end.
But there are also a lot of books.
All connecting to tell a never-ending story.
If you put them all together
They will do just that.
Libraries are eternal.
We're all together. Stacked.

Prana

I breathe the same air Huey Newton breathed.
Play the same guitar Jimi Hendrix played.
Study the same cosmos Neil Degrasse Tyson studies.
Feel the same pain Nina Simone felt.
I speak the same message Saul Williams speaks.
Fight the same hatred Bob Marley fought.
Awakening to the same morning you did today...
For, I am my ancestor's wildest dreams.
And, I breathe for them.

<u>**Live. Die.**</u>

Some people have all the money in the world
And, still have nothing.
Others have no material possessions
Yet have everything they need.
In a society that breeds egotism, unhealthy
attachments...
We must be mindful that...

Everything begins. Everything ends.
Everything changes.
People come. People go.
We give. We take.
We fuck up. We learn.
There are highs. There are lows.

Through it all,
Unwavering, immortal Love for Self must remain
constant.
You are truly all you have.
You live. You die.

The Darkness
Continuum

I had a meeting with the devil.

<u>Silent Lips</u>

I am afraid of the dark.
Nocturnal resistance.
Strong in my light.
Weak in my night.
She is my stalker.
My sleepless nights.
The moon is my friend.
My only strength.
With every sunset, I am hidden within myself.
She has x-ray vision.
Glaring through my fears.
Phobic tendencies.
The night shines with her whispers.
I kiss her silent lips.
The thrill trembles my fingertips.
Chills run down my spine.
I now see the beauty of such darkness.
Give in. Sink myself within.
Lack of oxygen.
Gasping breaths in and out to air.
The bittersweet taste of this suffocating black
Has become a parasite to my soul.
She is now in control.

Black soul. Black presence...
I am now one with the darkness.
I am known. I am present...
I am now one with the darkness.
Black soul. Black presence...
I am now one with the darkness.
I have become what I feared most.

Joann C. Roberts

<u>All is Well</u>

Dark days.
Bright nights.
Cannot rise with the Sun.
Cannot close eyes with the Moon.
White eyes...
Dark eternal.
Black eternally...
For eternity.
Misleading.
Mistreating.
This reading...
Is keeping...
Me bleeding...
Through vicious vaults.
Me feeding...
My morbid thoughts.
Tears through wrists...
Tightened   fists.
Cold   and   brisk...
Knife severed kiss.
Like a protected shell...
Of a deadly snail...
All is well...
In my hell.

<u>Big Black Revolver</u>

Big black revolver.

Big round bullets.

Pitch black darkness

Viewed in its fullest.

No shame in my aim.

Batter my brains.

Dim and dull.

Shatter my skull.

Big black revolver.

Big black pain.

Snap that trigger.

Stop flow in veins.

I take my life.

No vows to recite.

Flashy and sudden.

Head splitting...

Eye cutting.

Joann C. Roberts

Curled Fingernails

I am pure in this depression.
It reveals my true self.
I write with true pen.
For, it is the pen that helps.
I am trapped in a hole.
The hole of my soul.
That has control of my goal
To kill myself.
This is beautiful truth
My beautiful pain.
With fingernails curled
I tighten the chains.
I am going to kill myself.
Take a knife and peel myself.
Watch the blood drip
And, smile in this bliss.
The pain and sorrow
Will be the same tomorrow
Since I've blamed and followed
The plain and hollow.
I am pure in this depression.
It reveals my true self.
I write with true pen.
For, it is the pen that helps.

Death...
Escape from this prison.

<u>Mirror, Mirror</u>

I had a meeting with the devil.

His demons, too.

I approached him in darkness

With light beaming through.

No large horns. Just red eyes

That appeared to be gleaming through

My soul...

In which the eyes served no meaning to.

Surrounded by fire

With light streaming through.

I was fantasizing.

Must have been dreaming, too.

I stood there and stared.

Fearless to eyes gleaming through.

I started leaning.

He started leaning, too.

I was looking in the mirror.

Quicksand

Such potential to be detrimental to my credentials.

This is my potential. Essential.

My profound mental.

Open heart. Clear mind.

Magnifies this Entity.

Bright Sun. Closed Blinds.

Divine Symmetry.

This dream reality is only a fallacy to my mentality.

This dream reality. A Fallacy...

In all actuality.

Black Pen. Red Ink.

Written upon my face.

Introspect with cognitive ink...

Open and shut case.

This recommends that I extend my reprimands.

Beginning. No end.

The only way out is within.

Come... Go... Again...

Then again.

The uncatchable I am after.

Such a beautiful disaster.

I am sinking in the quicksand of my thoughts.

<u>Hope</u>

I wish I could confront my mistakes head on.
Go head to head with all regrets and get on with my life.
But, throughout my pain and strife
You have always crossed my mind.
Even when at times I tried to delete you
But, could not allow my heart to defeat you.
Even now I still keep you...
In my thoughts.
I used to dwell in all the naive things I did and said.
Afraid of seeing you again...
You may just see the old Joann...
When I have grown so much outside and within.

You say people come in and out of our lives for a reason
So, you don't feel the need for us to speak.
No use in provoking or hoping...
So, I'd lay broken and cut open...
From a friendship once at its peak.
You were relevant to my development
But, I was given no time for repentance...
When communication was immunization
For this sickness.
I still feel a connection to you
Despite our distance...
You were there for me in many ways on many days.
I miss you friend, and I can't express it enough.
Thank you for laying next to me on nights I was
Alone. Sick. Afraid.

If you ever need me, you'll know where to find me:
Running from all this darkness behind me.

<u>Train</u>

Can't have a bride without trust.

Can't do any healing without calm.

Yet in every corner is chaos.

Timeout.

Nowhere to face this wall built by

Demons.

These feelings hang heavy.

Keeping me from reaching the top.

Floating upward like a bubble.

Like the cream of the crop.

Just to be hit by another train.

Nonstop.

Blood Moon

It is her night sky I awaken to.
Her eclipse my eyes are taken to.
Our atmosphere is a filtered lens
For rising sons to get filtered in.
Daily battles of war and gunfights.
We stand in shadows and ignore the sonlight.
Preoccupied with the dark side of her moon
Brings hide tides on the shore for one night.
Flooding rooms with burning heads
Named "Blood Moon" for she's turning red.
Pay mind. No light on her surface.
So, setting sons get reflected instead.
Sis moon. Brother sun. Earth aligned.
Redshifts, Blueshifts from her spine.
Bringing tsunamis that make one SEEsick.
In the dawn of her Lunar Eclipse.
Daily battles of war and gunfights.
We stand in shadows and ignore the sonlight.
Preoccupied with the dark side of her moon
Brings hide tides on the shore for one night.
It is her night sky I awaken to.
Her occultation I am taken to.
Celestial bodies rotate on tilted bends
For rising sons that get filtered in.
Can't tell where she begins and we end.

Return...

Love is in the Earth.
Grass grows from soil...
Trees from roots...
Mountains from shifts.
We are born of this and we die of this...
Returning to Source...
We return to Love.
No need to fear death
If it is the last step.
Death is truly all we have left.

...Home

Sometimes I seek to return from which I came.
No pleasure. No pain.
No money. No fame.
No titles. No name.
No pride. No shame.
No guilt. No blame.
No calm. No strain.
No rules. No games.
No Sun. No rain.
No miss. No aim.
No picture. No frame.
No yin. No yang.
No sky. No terrain.
No words. No brain.
No heart. No veins...
Just the nothingness from which I came.

The Pen Helps

There once were days I couldn't get out of bed.

Divine Intervention

There once were days I couldn't get out of bed.
Brain dead... Ego fed...
Repetitive thoughts clouding my head.
I used to lie there and wonder why I was even alive...
I was so busy drowning in mental lakes and
being haunted by my mistakes.
I don't know what it means to be enlightened...
Just what it means to be frightened.
Blood boiling, pulse heightened...
Yet a million miles away from excitement.
Up until now I believed people like me
would always finish last.
Now I know why writing used to be illegal,
I managed to come across a pen and pad.
I don't think people understand why I write...
I'm not in the business of rhymes or riddles
and sharing my demons for shits and giggles.
Yeah, I'm in a sea full of other poets
and just drifting along with the tide,
But while some just write for money and pride,
the rest of us write to stay alive.
When I was twelve I told my father
I wanted to be an artist.
He got pissed and started crying...
So from then on I started lying... To myself.
I figured that life was all about wealth...
In a society where success is measured by your income.
So, in my world full of thunder my pen and pad got
quiet. I set my writing skills to the side.
Went to school and became a pilot.
But, my will to write only got stronger
so it wasn't much longer
Before beats became knowledge

and the streets became college.
I went from being a scholar
with a good job and expensive cars
To being paid in abundance
with nothing but a dream and my guitar.
Something had to be wrong with me
to choose a life among the hardest...
But this life chose me. It brings light to my darkness.
I decided not to be hesitant
with a gift that is heaven sent.
But they say that if it doesn't pay then it's irrelevant.
So, despite shedding blood, sweat, and tears...
I'm seen as just another nigga.
But anyone who thinks I'm worthless
just doesn't know I have a purpose.
I felt like I was standing in a forest
and no one else could see the trees
So I made the choice to be a voice for niggas like me.
There were mornings I didn't think
I would rise with the Sun.
The only other way to face my problems was to run.
I don't think people understand why I write...
I have love for slamming, don't get it twisted,
but this isn't about competitions.
I appreciate your scores and critiques of my technique...
But my poetry just is. I don't even need to speak.
I believe in the power of words
So I come with no performance tactics.
No special delivery package.
No gimmicks or stage theatrics.
I leave my ego at the door
and I'm just here to share my story.
I write for closure. Not exposure.
I'm just here to share my glory.
So, here I am, 15 years later,

after telling my father I'd be doing this.
I understand it was out of worry
that he tried to stop me from pursuing this.
Yet, here I am gracing this stage,
sharing my pain page for page...
'til I open up and become a vessel,
connecting lives like train trestles.
The Universe gave me the ink
so I dip it in those mental lakes.
Building bridges over water
to keep from drowning in my mistakes.
This is my mindful meditation...
My life story in non-fiction...
My IV for dehydration...
Therapy for my addictions.
This is the clearest I've been able to think...
The furthest I've been able to see...
The most I've ever been able to feel...
And, it brings me so much peace.
So, the next time someone mentions
the art of divine intervention...
Keep in mind some of us don't do this for attention.

Glass

I speak in shards of glass from the mirror...
I don't know where I'm going
but I know just where I've been.
Take my past, present, and future
then toss them into the wind...
Seeing before me a reflection of my imperfections.
"You're like a pearl in a shell"...
This is what the mirror tells.
Telling tales of mirrored jails refracting from cells.
I test my luck on broken glass...
Let the mirror give direction.
Beaming prisms that change
the complexion of my perception.
Scribing thoughts on mirrors
in this section of broken glass.
Shades of grey are now blurring my past.
Shuffling cards and bleeding from shards...
Keeping composure while searching for closure...
Seeing before me the reflection of my imperfections.
Think less. Feel more.
Rise again from broken glass
Sweep up the glass from the floor.
Think less. Feel more.
From glass that cuts away at your pores.
Put broken glass in the past
and lock it among steel doors.
Bend. Make amends...
That's what love of self is still for.
Think less. Feel more.
Wounds heal from shattered mirrors...
Even if fogged vision is clouding your cognition.
Think less, feel more.
Rise again from broken glass...
So, even in this inked mess you build more.

<u>Why I Write</u>

Poetry is art.
Art is subjective.
If the words reach your heart
Then we're all The Artist Collective.
Even though I am selective I appreciate this perspective.
I just don't like it when I am pressured to slam.
They say not every slam poet is a poet
And, not every poet is a slam poet.
I say, who is "they"? Although, I somewhat agree.
It's not necessarily the competition- it's the pressure...
Like, competing in front of the masses
is your rights of passage.
I'm not a poet if I don't slam.
It's not art if I don't perform.
I'm sorry... I wasn't aware competing is the norm.
Some Poets become egoic...
They write for attention and entertainment.
The audience is where they take their pen and aim it.
Not that this is a bad thing, I'm just apathetic to that.
I don't seek out scores and credits
for my message to be respected.
I'm not a 3-minute poet. My shit ends when I say so.
But there were a couple times
I've slammed just for the pesos.
If 3 minutes is all it takes to make sure
I have a place to sleep.
Then 3 minutes will be all it takes
to keep me on my own two feet.
I was once so distracted
that my self-expression was impacted...
Since I live in a society
demanding of education notoriety.
But in matters of intelligence
doing what you love is what's relevant.
Cause I got tired of 9 to 5s
and helping old White men stay rich.

I admit I've won a few slams to financially stay alive...
Slam is an expression, it's just not where I thrive.
I've experienced pain so unbearable,
I'd become hysterical.
And, writing all through those days
helped me crawl through the maze.
So, if you expect me to just slam
then I am not the poet for you.
I'm a writer first and foremost.
This I know to be true.
A lot of those poets sound the same.
Their delivery is typical.
And, they often demand support that isn't reciprocal.
I prefer open mics. I don't care for competition.
I just seek to give words life, like an obstetrician.
For, some experience stage fright in their everyday life
And, there are those who can't tell their story, but I can.
So, in all fairness I wrote this for suicide awareness
Cause today we woke up wanting to die.

I write. I share. For us.

Today we woke up wanting to die.

<u>Remnants</u>

Remnants of my descendants

lie within my independence.

With every sentence that is written,

I remind them of this difference.

Write!

If you ask what inspires me.
I'll say "Everything that tires me".
So I clutch the pen to touch within...
Because, I write toward a higher me.
Why do we eat? Why do we breathe? I ask you.
The same reasons I write. I have to.
I write for social justice;
cause sometimes I feel it's just us.
And, this pen is my riot
in a society too complacent and quiet.
So, I write for those who can't write.
I write for those who can't speak.
Especially, for those no longer here
by the hands of crooked police.
If art is the voice of the masses...
Then there is no "me" without "you".
If art is the voices of our ashes
I do all my ancestors weren't allowed to.
So, I write for those who can't fight.
I write for those who can't eat.
Especially for those who couldn't be here
cause they're out surviving on the streets.
I write poetry because doing so helps me sleep at night.
I write for those in darkness
who need help to see the light.
I write to reflect an amazing universe that designed me
And, allows me to write myself
out of boxes that attempt to define me.
There are thousands who can't
speak for me and yet they still try.
So, I write for self-awareness
cause no one knows me better than I.
I write as if healing from the inside out
is all I know how to do
Despite never quite hearing the words
"I'm proud of you".
I'll have folks sipping on these nouns
and tasting on these verbs.
It may appear I'm wasting words
but I'm awakening your nerves.
If art serves as a mirror,
then it should reflect us at our best.

For, words will live longer than flesh
and remain well beyond death.
I write for little black boys and girls
forced to play dangerous games of hide and seek.
I write for the letters L G B and T...
For us... gender benders and "freaks"...
I write because we're a part of a system
that prefers to pretend we don't exist.
But I'm here... and I write for them
to know our pains and strengths.
I write on buses, at slams, and retreats.
I write for... cyphers, battles, and beats.
Most importantly, I write for freedom,
for truth, and for peace.
Poetry can pay the bills if you take time
to weigh your skills
But, what does that matter
if you never use the stage as a way to build?
No slam titles or just to perform.
I write to make rose petals of my thorns.
I write to break ground, combat oppression,
and challenge societal norms.
I write when suicidal. I write to release.
I write for you. I write for my niece.
I write to question authority.
I'd much rather that than watch TV.
I write for those who think they're better writers
and I tell them to keep dreaming.
I scribe my thoughts before sunrise
so I can stand behind them by evening.
Poetry itself doesn't save lives
but it attests to my will to survive.
This is so much more
than a chance to speak my opinions and rant.
Artists, you are free to do whatever pleases you.
But whatever it be that inspires you
I hope it leads to a higher you.
There is no one we can trust
to tell our own stories but us.
So, "Speak poet!". I write because I must.

A Poem That Writes Itself

I worry the only title I can have is "Poet".
Everywhere else I'm too stoic and I know it.
Maybe it's because I was meant to be a loner.
A traveling, meditating, poetry writing stoner.
I don't like it when people say Art doesn't save lives.
Literally, no but figuratively this is so.
Poetry is my manifesting a spiritual form
for every death upon death 'til I'm spiritually born.
With poetry I can reach up and hug the stars.
Profess my heart to Saturn and make love to Mars
I can... walk on Andromeda and dance with comets.
Kiss lips of Dark Matter
and grace Mercury with sonnets.
I didn't realize how much was wrong with the world
until I picked up a pen and paid mind.
I didn't realize how much was right with the Sun
until it disappeared in the daytime.
I'm the living proof of my written truths.
I'd lose my mind without a sense of these words.
With letters I mold keys to deepen my thoughts.
Wrapping words to curves on keys to these vaults.
"Poetry does this. Poetry does that.
Poetry ain't this. Poetry ain't rap."
I say Art is love and Art is life...
And, it has a way of bringing the best out of you.
Words have range and can never be changed...
They can only be transferred.
At times we may forget the wordsmith
But, we will never forget the words.
I didn't realize just how beautiful life could be
until I picked up a pen and started writing.
So, if a poet is a all I am, then Ase'.
For, I am a poem that is writing itself...

"A poem requires an eternity before and after it" –Unknown

Cliché Slam Poem

I do this poetry shit cause I love it.
And, these are skills that I build
so people can covet my words
and feel what it is that I do.
You are me and I am you but this shit is my drug.
This is my antiseptic I rub and scrub it all over my soul
when I have wounds I need to heal.
And when there are tombs I need to fill
I go ahead and take action
'cause I kill on the mic, I'm just keeping it real.
Hip hop is the love of my life but, I'm playing the field
cause spoken word is my mistress;
I consider this to be business.
'Cause for as long as I could remember,
January through December,
I've been writing these rhymes
and reciting these lines
about my life and these times on paper.
Treating the library like a gym.
Getting brolic with this knowledge.
I never grasped guns in these fists of fury.
I used to walk thru the hood
grasping a dictionary and, a thesaurus.
'Cause these nouns and verbs
become sounds and words to my weaponry.
I used to commit felonies at spelling bees.
So, ain't no telling me that words don't have power.
'Cause when it comes to the eleventh hour
all you have is your word.
I've served time for these heard lines.
Only gotten arrested for my diction.
I've maintained by battles.
I used to gangbang on Scrabble.

Going to war with any star like a Jedi.
Leaving people with red eyes
like night flights across the Pacific Ocean.
Rhyming in a specific motion
I put in work 24 hours a day, 7 days a week,
I'm rhyming and timing words,
even writing in my sleep.
I be wildin' when I'm spitting.
Never freestylin' any writtens.
And, if you think you're compatible I'll battle you.
Not an attack. Nothing personal.
I'm just better with the letters.
I eat alphabet soup for breakfast
while everyone else is chasing cheddar.
Crackling toes and ruffling feathers
When it comes to this text.
I wake up every morning
and write a song or two before I stretch.
A___year old vet, I be on some other shit.
I'm from fucking outer space,
I communicate for my mother ship.
Putting altruism to a rhythm cause I master within.
Call me a warden with these bars
cause I master the pen.
If I don't win who cares I'll keep my chin in the air.
All I need to get through the day is a pen and a snare.
Through days and days of time,
I got pages and pages of rhymes.
I just wrote this to let you know... The stage is mine.

The Haunting

They sneak in through the back door.
Stand over me while I am sleeping.
They infiltrate my dreams.
Invade my guards. Security weakening.
They kiss me in the morning.
Greet me with ideas of creations.
In my head they are always forming.
Pulling from everyday conversations.
They haunt me by way of billboards.
Walls, fliers, letters, signs. Books.
They lay hidden within the city's graffiti
Anchoring my ships by way of hooks.
They then set me off to sea.
Breaking chains while wave gliding.
As a slave to them I am free.
Guiding my ancestors to new horizons.
Shedding boundaries and pushing envelopes
They take me far beyond the Cosmos.
They remind me of where I'm from
Painting identities beyond Chicago.
They haunt me in the darkness
Brush along my shoulder when in anguish.
They abduct me onto their starships
In light of teaching me their Love language.
Giving lessons in my depression
Bringing blessings in all I lack.
They take my fears and they disappear.
Only to never give them back.
They're in the forests and in the trees.
They're in the mountains and in the seas.
They are all I wish them to be.
Words are you. Words are me.

Can't help it when it comes to words,
'cause words help me.

he(art)

Art takes
Away from heartbreak
Yet, still my heart aches
For Freedom

Auburn Gresham

I come from where people hustle
And, young black men get into trouble.
Where buildings collapse to nothing everyday
And, we search for our dreams in the rubble.
I said "One day I'll be free from this"
But these chains, they tend to follow.
Not physically, but mentally
And, that pain makes me a model.
What to do but keep ascending?
With the blood sweat and tears of my ancestors.
Passing the torch along back home.
Ridding broken souls of all that can fester.
So, if I killed myself today
The world would still be as troubled tomorrow.
And, there would be one less person
To show the beauty that comes from Chicago.

Words from Saturn

There is a skeleton in my closet.

Skeletons

There is a skeleton in my closet.
Behind the confines of my mind
It rests.
At peace with its own secrets.
Where dreams are tied to shackles
Hoisting baggage upon broken axles.
Like a strung-out horse I drag these loads
up each hill in desperation.
Sweaty palms and dirty nails...
Chaotic heavens and sturdy hells.
I have died many deaths...
Having been at a loss of many breaths.
Noticing that any step
I take on this road less traveled
Leaves the sun cooking away at my imperfections,
Charring my feet upon this gravel.
And, I am not a camel,
Having not been designed to withstand this type of heat.
Therefore, I've avoided many kitchens,
many deserts, and every beach.
Extend my arms out in front of me
for all that lies beyond my reach
I was... too busy trying to teach
rather than practicing what I preach.
So I... drag my feet
Up these hills in perspiration.
This is now a matter of survival.
A "She has no vitals" type revival.
And, given these events I know
that I must consent to all hints.
I occupy a mind and body in this space...
Therefore, I must pay rent.
I've lit a fire, now I'm choking for air.

I've blown a tire but I have a spare.
Having chosen to address my attitude
I look to now finesse my gratitude.
No more walking on stained glass.
Awaiting this pain to pass.
I am the reason for the season
And, it is time to get this hot sun off of my ass.
I was bound by my own chains,
Not knowing what it meant to be free.
Too busy trying to construct a path
that was already built for me.
So, I... move along now up this hill in aspiration.
Such a struggle was my destiny
Among many lessons experience meant to be.
I let go of all attachments.
Bid farewell to all distractions.
Life happens...
And time flies... but, I'm the captain.
Less speech, more action,
As I leave this baggage where it is supposed to be.
Behind me, I see...
I can move along now more easily.
All this time I thought I was cursed
But the Universe just reimbursed...
To me.
The wisdom and strength it takes to know
I should always put me first.
So, I... run full speed tackling these hills in celebration.
I now see life for what it is,
It is time to Love. Laugh. Live.
Let go.

<u>Change</u>

I am sensitive to my mind.
It's unknown and its thoughts.
Against my will
I give into my intellectual tendencies and faults.
My heart is weak in many beats.
It is racing as I am pacing.
Stripped of my pride I run and hide.
From situations I am facing.
Impatience is awakened.
Aching in a soul that needs maintenance.
Giving or taking this education.
Wasting courses I should be acing.
Conscience is born from right and wrong experiences...
Fearing its persuasion through a clearance.
Gained by my appearance.
Reluctant advances call
for a tortured mind through time.
Hesitant reactions as a result of given time in my mind.
Difficult to comply. My replies I deny.
I am giving into objects on the ground
rather than the wonder in the sky.
Responsible brain in opposition to a youthful heart.
Pain arrives in sequence only to never finish from start.
In my unconscious I gather the results strategically.
Only to find my life, perceptions, and values
all lack in decency.

This is my testimonial secrecy.
I must grow. I must change.

<u>Alive</u>

Sometimes I need the morning sun
To reassure myself that I, too, can rise.
I, too, can shine and give life...
Having been born from forever.

Sometimes I need the mountains
So that I may bask in the beauty of Earth's design.
Realizing that life too goes up and down...
Yet never loses its awe.

Sometimes I need to see the stars
To remind me what I am made of.
Where I come from...
My place in this universe...
And just how precious we all are.

Sometimes I need the clouds
To remind me of times I've flown in and out of them.
Extend my hand...
Be closer to heaven...
The sky hugging my finger tips.

Sometimes I need the wind
To lift me up when I am down.
To keep me grounded when too high...
I fly...
Listening to the trees.

Sometimes I need my mother's touch.
The way she looks at me says enough.
Unconditional love...
Her willingness to be my spine...
Even at her weakest.
Sometimes I need to dream
To better fathom my reality.
For it is not easy to separate the two...
When you dream as hard as I.

Sometimes I need poetry
To warm my heart when it is cold.
The pen and pad,
Energy exposed...
Balancing my soul in the Universe.

Sometimes I need love
Just to know that it is real.
For I doubt when I am without...
Trusting that I will someday love, again.

Sometimes I need the mirror
To know that I am me.
My brown skin...
Full of asymmetry...
Learning to love my reflection.

Sometimes I need to see the eyes of children
Witness their innocence.
Their worry free lives.
Joy in life's simple things...
Taking a lesson from their purity.

Sometimes I need my grandmother's picture
To remember the last time she held me.
The times she has visited me since...
I reminisce...
Providing me comfort in times of fear.

Sometimes I need this moment
To understand the past.
How it will affect my future
Living in the now...
And, appreciating these times.

I then can grasp why it is so wonderful...
To just BE.

<u>Underwhelmed. Overstand.</u>

As I push the boundaries of all that is real and possible...
These times and moods call for solitude.
Shining light onto my insecurities...
Decided to face the fear in me.
So, I stand before mental mirrors stripped totally nude.

Having missed many sunrises and sunsets...
I missed church on Sunday
And, just landed on a dark runway.
Of a deserted airport
To detest wounds of impending doom.
Past ahead of me, future behind...
Infesting the vitality of my own mind.

Now third eye blind...
I am prisoner to my mind.
Having succumbed to the indolence of
Long days and short nights.
Much too tedious to put up a fight.
Yet, despite I still fight.
Conscious of my efforts to give
To all of me that is positive.

Another law-abiding victim
Confined to a system...
That I have allowed to define my existence.
Too caught up in bills, bank accounts,
degrees and flight fees.
Too worried about elected presidents
To acknowledge my own resonance.
Newly found sensations now provide me obligations
To put meditation before medication
And, Universal Law before man.
Manifest my success, for it is all in my hands.
Underwhelmed by this,
I overstand.

Japan

I used to go to the beach in my attempt to reach
The Divine.
Where mountains grew from water
and the sea appeared to align...
With the sky, so I'd try to find strength in a sun
That never seemed to shine enough
and hardly ever seemed to come.
I was unable to comprehend as to why my best friend
Was the Moon.
I'd stare at it from my room,
While sulking in the darkness of my days.
I used to look up at the stars
and beg to return from which I came.
I had taken a turn for the worst
and sought to rid myself of the pain.
When I first got on that plane
I was sure I'd never be the same.
Running from life, running from love,
in my attempt to displace the blame.
"Daijobu desuka?" My sister-in-law would ask.
Assuring her I was okay,
almost as though I was protecting my mask.
The mask I hid behind
that did not allow me to face my fears.
I went to temples, I went to shrines...
but, they failed to stop the tears.
Until one day I just decided...
To take my mind and divide it...
Among my Self. Cause, I was all I had left.
"You are not your thoughts, so just let them be...
Practice Zen, construct a trend.

Celebrate this chance to be"
I then found myself at a place to trace my spirit faith.
Where mountains grew from water
and a sea appeared to align...
With the sky, so I tried to find strength in a sun
That never seemed to shine enough,
and hardly ever seemed to come.
I made a trip to Japan for I simply did not have a plan.
But the Universe only made me face
that from which I ran.
It may seem simplistic, but if one remains optimistic...
Taking your life into your hands
is the only way to understand,
Why the Moon was my best friend,
while I prayed to stars that never end.
It was reflecting light from the Sun
to remind me I am One...
With those mountains that grew from water
and a sea that appeared to align...
With the sky so I tried to find strength in the Sun.
Realizing that my body and the stars
contain the same elements.
Reminding me to remind my Self of this,
Whenever I have to question my relevance.

I found an inner peace in Japan.

The Sun (Part 2)

I woke up dead this morning.
I arose from the dead when I laid my head
to rest last night.
No roses grow from the ground over here.
I don't capitalize on the bits of soil
that exist between the cracks
Of my concrete thoughts.
I have buried myself.
Stuck between the Sun and the Moon
where I have to choose
Whether or not I want to be a source of light
Or simply a reflection.
And, this gravitational pull keeps me grounded.
But I don't allow the ground to blind me
from wonders of the sky...
So, I dream that I have wings.
Visiting places in my consciousness
Astronauts have never seen.
I've astral projected to Jupiter's many moons
and danced on Saturn's rings.
What we perceive as solid matter
is really just empty space.
We are everything there is,
yet nothing less and nothing more.
So, what are we here for?
Why should we have to go through a life
where we are victims to our limitations,
Wants, needs, and affirmations?
So, I cry when babies are born
and I smile when people die,
Cause they're free.
Just as I wish to be.
But the Sun never stops shining
It rises just when the night
is at its darkest with perfect timing...
Then I'm reminded.

That I am a reflection of a beautiful experience
the Universe has granted me...
In a way that I can just be.
And, listen to trees bend with the invisible wind.
Watch snow form on mountaintops
as rivers flow in sync with my tears.
Listen to waves crash on the coast just before a storm.
Then, I know I am just as precious as the Sun.

I've died and am here again. I've lived many times so...
Rebirth of life brings new beginnings
when we embrace endings.
And, as I begin this new journey among the stars
I reminisce on how life was once so lifeless.
Love told me she was used to walking
alongside the Sun.
And, that's why when she touched me
my insides burned so immensely.
"Fear not the fire, nor the flames", she said...
"This is thermodynamic.
Join me in the Sun"
Cause, the Sun never stops shining
It rises just when the night
is at its darkest with perfect timing.
And, I am reminded...
That she is a reflection of a beautiful experience
the Universe has granted me,
in a way that we can just be.
And, listen to trees bend with the invisible wind.
Watch snow form on mountaintops
as rivers flow in sync with my tears.
And, I know that when the Sun rises tomorrow
We'll be the first flower after the flood.

<u>Mother</u>

One day my sky will break
and all within me will escape...
For eyes are the soul...
And, mine are dark and eternal.
Karma police, arrest me. I am in need of an escape.
Serving time for a curving mind...
Correct and facilitate my fate.
Cold hearted. I was born in the mental state of Illinois.
To connect with humanity, I rely on tears for my sanity.
In mental rooms I play with zoom,
looking through the lens of my camera.
Trying to capture the demons that await me in Montana.
Mental rebirth, I know is...
Essential research to my growth.
Serving as a portal to the truth...
And, how I am immortal to my youth.
Black holes have sucked away my soul
and I am told that I did it.
I am good at killing myself,
but no such crime has been committed.
Still, I seek imprisonment...
With spirit robbed by ego greed.
Still, I seek imprisonment
For, one must be trapped to be freed.
Heavy like metal...
I rebirth and curve the edges of metallic beams.
For this wisdom is woman...
And, it is through her wombs that I am cleansed.

<u>Colors</u>

I am trying to create new paintings from an ego dead.
Trying to turn black to red
but only getting brown instead.
Grounded in my root chakra,
I chant 3rd eye mantras...
While the ego tells me I am nothing without it.
Nothing without it. Everything is about it.
So, I "Om" on colors to free myself,
But, purple tells me otherwise.
I see the shine in my mother's eyes.
Earth aura energy field.
It is the color of my aura among the absence of light.
Red chakra for passion.
Orange chakra for addictions...
My desire is to be grounded,
yet closer to the source of energy.
Pastel sensitivity...
Meditate on sacral and roots.
Scribing in my heart and centering in on sacral truths.
Every morning I walk further away from me
between shades of black.
My aura turns black and black is the absence of color.
Black is beautiful in higher dimensions.
Yellow creativity in my intentions.
With heart and throat chakra awareness
Comes 3rd eye vision "repairment".
I grow with green light for contentment.
Third eye indigo dark for resentment.
I meditate on cool and calm
with the universe in my palms...
I breathe in peace to the blue.
All colors come splashing through.
Silver aura for awakening the cosmic mind.
Gold aura for highest good,
I awaken through cosmic time.
As the color white purifies my mental light,
I breathe out...
Letting the pain go.
Chakra colors of the rainbow.

Dear Universe:

With an energy field glow.
You creep into dark rooms.
Among the weak, the bad, and the heartless.
Those who find comfort in darkness.
I have been waiting for you...
Among nightmares and dreams that were lucid.
Wide awake, restless nights.
Yet, too serene to give into Cupid.
We are the ones who learned the hard way,
Arrows aim to hearts that die often.
We find and lose ourselves in others
For we lie in these self-made coffins.
With energy field glow
My deaths receive a taste of your essence.
I am now yet another heart given life
By the starlight of your fluorescence.

OM

I take a second to breathe
And, be conscious of my breath.
Take steps to raise awareness
While being conscious of the steps.
I'm in my body, feel my feet.
Feel my fingers and hands.
Time my heart, feel the beat
As my lungs collapse and expand.
Align my chakras. Relax my shoulders.
Feel my bones through their components.
I chant mantras as I get older
To be mindful of the moments.
In and out, between the chaos
I breathe in my full worth.
I'm an expansion. A manifestation.
I am the light of the universe.

Of My Mother (I Am)

I am a...

Free spirited

Free-thinking

Free body

Vegan eating

Dread loc growing

Guitar string knowing

Drum playing

Poetry saying

Plane flying

Mountain climbing

Star chasing

World racing

Higher level

Hippie rebel

Woman lover

From another.

I Am...

Of my mother.

Paradise

These recreation times should be vacation times.
Yet, I occupied my mind with rhymes of crime.
I could not find my mind...
To see the world, I was blind.
Count to ten. I'd only make it 9.
I've got to get away. I can't fake it this time.
This is my vacation time.
Mind vacation time.

Mr. Postman

I was brainwashed, but that isn't the proper term.
I only washed my brain to clear my head.
Stop the pain as I watch this train
Barrel through my tunnel visions
On these one track mind type rails.
Moving along like snails.
Cruising along like sails.
Losing my mail cause what gets delivered isn't mail.
Dear Postman, I have wings. I need an address change.
Through freight trains and rough terrains...
Pushing envelopes through mailboxes.

Barefoot

Driving on roads and paying tolls.
Pathways that never end.
I know where I want to be... Eventually.
Too busy looking through my rearview
to see what lies in front of me.
But I'm running low on gas and time is kicking my ass.
I keep remembering my past and forgetting my future.
Can't change lanes and merge
so I just ride along the curb.
Plenty of time for pit stops in order to rest and digest.
This road is never ending and was not paved for me.
Park the car for I finally understand...
Life can only be lived now and understood backwards.
I see mountains worth journeying off road
for new chapters.
I get out of the car...
And, walk toward them.

Love's Lead

Where is Love?
I can't seem to find it.
With mind in heart and no brain, I never mind it.
I drive a night desert third eye blinded.
Walking in Love's shadow...
I learn to stand behind it.

Balance

When I go one way the other side pulls me back.
When I avoid derailment I still fall off track.
I'm... balancing this hourglass of my past on a scale.
Teetering and tottering between my freedom and jail.
I'm a fence sitter...
Trying to bring players round home base
like a pinch hitter.
Love is hard but life is even harder.
I bet my father never thought
he'd have a Sun for a daughter.
I... martyr and barter with my physicality,
Crucifying man's truth-defying slave mentality.
I'm in one of many galaxies as an addict of women.
Lighted room of spirituality, yet the bulb is dimming.
Messing around with these women
left my cranium spinning.
Still running circles through 20 innings.
I need to love myself before I can love anyone else,
Just as I value my health more than my wealth.
I am... balancing my power in the Sun's hands.
Wondering why the people
give so much power to one man.
Presidents are not your leaders.
Value lies not in sneakers.
And, believe it or not, you are your brother's keeper.
One foot in. One foot out on the grass.
And, mowing lawns of pros and cons.
With this game getting older
And, many standing on my shoulders,
I call my final lap on this quest for balance.

Spirit Science

Spirit (Starseed):

Through brown eyed reflector frames
You need heart telescopes to see her planets.
Seeing beyond shades of black and white.
Where things that appear can quickly vanish.
The philosophy of her astronomy
Is quintessential to my mental.
And, the victims of her systems
Become universally exponential.
Blueshifting toward timelessness
Bound for answers via astral shuttles.
Human pain Earth wrapped in silences.
Settled heart through the eyes of Hubble.
There is no God but "God".
No beginning or end to my cosmic glow.
As below so above and beyond.
I went inside in order to know.

Science (Astronaut):

Through man-made refractor frames
We see her in shades of Black and white.
Need mind telescopes to view her planets.
She extends beyond our lack of sight.
The economy of her astronomy
Is quintessential to our potential
And, the systems of her wisdom
Are mathematically exponential.
Redshifting toward mindlessness.
Bound for answers via our shuttles.
Human pain Earth lacking kindnesses. Settled
minds through the eyes of the Hubble.
There is no God but "God".
No beginning or end to this cosmic show.
As below so above and beyond.
We had to go in order to know.

<u>Feel</u>

I feel good.

I feel great.

I feel I should.

I feel I'll wait.

I feel luck.

I feel sounds.

I feel up.

I feel down.

I feel closed.

I feel open.

I feel whole.

I feel devotion.

I feel regret.

I feel free.

I feel worry.

I feel me.

<u>Mars Retrograde</u>

I've had jobs galore
But have never worked this hard before.
I bow and nod to the floor
Welcoming the God of War.
Where no rotation is typical
He retrogrades between parallels.
We ride along on ellipticals
A merry-go-round of sun carousels.
The month of March for matriarchs
A gift of spring for kings and queens.
Bringing abilities of fertility
Yet cries of war begin to sing.
War within you. War within me.
A battle that rings serene.
War within youth. War within trees.
Cutting down the dreams of queens.
Circular motions of mental oceans.
Soaking woodpeckers in toppling trees.
Songs and tunes for wolves and moons.
Howling away at the monster in me.
Bringing abilities of tranquility.
Worshipping the God of spring.
From sterility to fertility.
Giving birth to the God in me.

(Mars is named for Mars, the God of war.
God of spring, growth, nature and fertility.
Its sacred animals are the wolf and woodpecker
and wars started or renewed in spring.)

Green Light (4 AM)

Another sleepless night
Being woken up at the crack of dawn
Cracking through the dawn of my evolution.
Light shines through cracks in my seclusion.
Ridding me of all confusion
A grip once so tight now loosened.
Spirit guide standing in the corner...
Once invisible now translucent.
Pictures of freedom fighters on my alter
Asking me "What are you waiting for?"
"The work has been done.
All you have to do is manifest!"
That monster in you will be killed and put to rest.
Another sleepless night.
Ancestors knocking at my eyelids.
Tears I can't explain tell me I have nothing to fear.
So, here I am writing down what I already know.
I've been activated. Green light.
Go.

Within

I am a burning heat in winter
With healing at the center
This is passion for beginners
Where evolution is the winner.
With no boundaries, I enter...
A Trailblazer. Hell-raiser.
A Freedom Fighter
Down to my Spirit and Black anatomy.
A Life academy is my strategy
So go to class and pass this math
Of the path we all have...
Toward Love and Transcendence.
Cause, everything is about "God".
Not about money or image.
When you find the God/Goddess in you...
You'll get it.

Fatigue (It's Time)

Man, I'm tired.
Woke up this morning in realization
Did morning meditations, rolled a joint,
and poured libations...
For my creator,
cause I often question the maker of men.
Yet I get that I'll never get it
So, I take my thoughts to paper and pen.
In daily life I find myself in dire need of frequent breaks
I'm exhausted,
playing along with this endless game of give and take.
I get tired of following rules
without regard to truly living.
My shovel just comes up empty
but here I am digging and digging.
I live in a society dominated by patriarchy.
Where money is the only language
and you're invisible if you're artsy.
I'm tired of fitting in. Of being told I have to fit in.
That a certain form of social norms
should be Gold when it isn't.
Many know how it feels to try and build and get stuck.
To be dealt a hand of cards
they have to deal with little luck.
Not enough money for everyone
but college is everything.
Selling illusions of the material things
that all imperial brings.
Yes I get tired of my own contributing to their demise.
Generational trauma is real. We're hurting but we rise.
I'm tired of working to pay bills.
Tired of working and staying still.
Tired of being told

the only solution on Earth is taking pills.
At times we must remember
that even healers need therapy.
I get tired of social media
and pressure to compete for popularity.
I come from nothing.
A neighborhood of poverty and gang violence.
Where descendants of slaves and kings
roam the streets in pained silence.
Stalking paths straight and narrow,
shooting bullets through a barrel.
They'll run up on you in black apparel.
With mask on to hide the pharaoh.
But I get tired of running
after mirages of a life that doesn't exist.
Being bombarded with constant delusions of race,
gender, and politics.
I no longer know whom to trust,
I don't know what I mean when I say "Us".
Not just the police. Everywhere I turn
someone's trying to put me in their cuffs.
Being confined and misunderstood
leaves me escaping to the exit.
I'm tired of dating and relating
cause I'm tired of having exes.
But I know now
nothing awakens consciousness more than suffering.
For, any path worth healing on
is one paved by rediscovery.
Cause I'm tired of fighting Self
and not giving all to my craft.
Of the constant perception I have
that the water glass is only half...

So, its time to give back to me.
To heal and rebuild my communities.
Stop focusing on all that is lacking
unless I see it as opportunity.
It's time to stop seeking reciprocity
and let the Universe replenish me.
Take care of my own heart
and let Art provide Nature's energy.
I'll flow more freely like water
and spend more time on mountain peaks.
It's time to stop complaining
and relate my actions to my speech.
It is time to give way to having my own power over me.
Letting no outside projections
or perceptions tower over me.
Self-actualization. Have relations only of honesty.
Wealth Actualization. Consciously and responsibly.
Cause my ancestors were tired enough.
My grandmothers were tired of enough.
My mother is tired enough.
And, they've all sacrificed for my freedom.
I'm tired of not knowing my power
and giving way to the same shit.
It's time for some motherfucking changes.
Today, I claim it.

<u>Mantra</u>

I am healed.

I am forgiving.

I am forgiven.

I am better.

I am ready.

I am free.

I am disciplined.

I am focused.

I am wealthy.

I am smart.

I am healthy.

I am strong.

I am talented.

I am a pilot.

I am a leader

I am a parent

I am a life partner

I am here

I am home.

I am cosmic.

I am the Universe.

I give myself permission to be.

When all is said and done, it's not.

<u>Saturn Return</u>

When all is said and done, it's not.
I am crossing thresholds
into the next stage of my existence.
From a Pagan to Carl Sagan...
Stephen Hawking to Richard Dawkins...
We all just serve as vessels to universal echo.
Yesterday, forward. Tomorrow, backward.
All we have is now, or do we?
This is life in the times of science
Where we are slaves to political giants
And, fall victim to defiance of religious tyrants.
He comes around again
and makes his timely revolution.
Influencing our lives and our evolution.
Guiding us into safe haven from all of man's pollution.
True karma at which there is no substitution.
We are guided by celestials
Whom we define as extraterrestrials.
Yet there are those like me
who serve as vessels to their echo.
He masters his surroundings and our lives within.
We share with him in helium and hydrogen.
These are words from Saturn.
I serve as a vessel to his echo.

He speaks to me in universal language
With love that is free and untainted.
Guiding me through body and mind...
At points where all spirits intertwine...
And, helping me to find words I can never find.
As I embrace this journey
with the help of my spirit guide
I am grounded in his return
as another chance to be alive.
31. 32. 33. 34...
He closes doors and opens many more.
No place to be judges.
He teaches not to hold grudges...
For, every time he comes around I am forced to let go.
We are heavy in the physical,
carrying the weight of our demise.
Unaware we're wrapped
in beautiful blankets of the spirit skies.
He has returned to show me I am worthy.
27. 28. 29. 30.
Given the painful bliss of his lessons, I transcend...
So, thank you, Saturn...
Thank you for coming around, again.

"We are made of star stuff. We are a way for the cosmos to know itself. " – Carl Sagan

Follow Paradigm!

www.meetparadigm.com
www.facebook.com/meetparadigm
www.meetparadigm.bandcamp.com
www.soundcloud.com/meetparadigm
www.instagram.com/paradigmthejovian

Bookings & Contact: meetparadigm@aol.com
& joann.roberts15@gmail.com

Copyright © 2018 Joann C. Roberts

Made in the USA
Columbia, SC
29 June 2024

37713760R00157